MY
STORY
YOUR
GLORY

MY
STORY
YOUR
GLORY

BY MATTHEW WEST
WITH MATT LITTON

K-LOVE
BOOKS

FRANKLIN, TENNESSEE

K-LOVE. BOOKS

5700 West Oaks Blvd.
Rocklin, CA 95765

Published by K-LOVE Books/EMF Publishing, an imprint of Forefront Books. Distributed by Simon & Schuster.

Printed in the United States of America.

First edition: 2024
10 9 8 7 6 5 4 3 2 1

ISBN: 978-1-63763-310-6 (Hardcover)
ISBN: 978-1-63763-311-3 (E-book)

Library of Congress Control Number: Applied for

Cover Design by Bruce Gore, Gore Studio, Inc.
Interior Design by PerfecType, Nashville, TN

DEDICATION

This book is dedicated to Joe and Sharon West.
Mom and Dad, you are both a big inspiration
for the words on these pages.
You are the embodiment of what it looks like
to live our stories for God's glory.
I'm blessed to be your son.
—MW

CONTENTS

Introduction   9

DAY 1   My Life Story, Your Glory   17

DAY 2   My Identity, Your Glory   23

DAY 3   My Purpose, Your Glory   29

DAY 4   My Service, Your Glory   37

DAY 5   My Trust, Your Glory   45

DAY 6   My Courage, Your Glory   51

DAY 7   My Shame, Your Glory   59

DAY 8   My Thoughts, Your Glory   65

DAY 9   My Dependence, Your Glory   71

DAY 10   My Praise, Your Glory   77

DAY 11   My Patience, Your Glory   83

DAY 12   My Giving, Your Glory   89

DAY 13   My Forgiveness, Your Glory   95

DAY 14   My Priorities, Your Glory   101

DAY 15   My Broken Road, His Glory   107

DAY 16   My Freedom, Your Glory   113

DAY 17   My Promises, His Glory   119

DAY 18   My Past, Your Glory   125

DAY 19   My Memory, Your Glory   131

DAY 20   My Prayers, Your Glory   137

DAY 21   My Battles, Your Glory   143

DAY 22   My Rest, Your Glory   149

DAY 23   My Imperfections, Your Glory   155

DAY 24   My Belonging, Your Glory   161

DAY 25   My Contentment, Your Glory   167

DAY 26   My Revisions, Your Glory   173

DAY 27   My Legacy, His Glory   179

DAY 28   My Suffering, Your Glory   185

DAY 29   My Future, Your Glory   191

DAY 30   My Hope, Your Glory   197

Acknowledgments   203

About the Author   204

INTRODUCTION

Years ago, I took a road trip from my hometown near Chicago, Illinois, back to my new home of Nashville, Tennessee. I had made that drive hundreds of times before and knew the directions like the back of my hand. But as the hours passed, I daydreamed (as songwriters tend to do). As I daydreamed, I drifted. And as I drifted, I unknowingly missed my exit and began heading off course. It wasn't until I noticed a highway sign welcoming me to Memphis, Tennessee, that I realized I had driven over three hours in the wrong direction. My absentmindedness and one wrong turn left me lost, confused, and desperately trying to find my way back to where I belonged.

I have learned that the stories of our lives can be like a road trip in that way. We can easily lose the truth of our story, take our eyes off the destination, and drift off course.

I first discovered the power of a story growing up in the front-row pew of my dad's church. He was a great storyteller and had a special way of connecting the stories of our lives with the greater story that God has been telling throughout history. Some of the most compelling moments of sermons I heard growing up were accounts of God working in incredible ways through the lives of His people.

Like my dad, I've become a storyteller too. From the first time I sat down with that old guitar in my room, I knew my mission in life would be to tell stories, one three-minute song at a time. Many of the songs that mean the most to me are based on true stories of the people I have met along my journey. There is nothing more inspiring and uplifting than witnessing how God is at work in people's lives. Our testimonies of God's faithfulness have the power to embolden one another, carry one another through hard times, and change the world.

And that is the purpose of the book you hold in your hands right now.

This is a devotional about *your* story. It is a guide to help you remember that your life is being written by the Master Storyteller and that you are here on this earth for an important reason: to give God glory. Just like my surprising road trip to Memphis, our stories can head in the wrong direction if we take our eyes off home. The enemy would love for nothing more than to distract you from your life's purpose. You see, he also has a plan for your story. He seeks to distract, discourage, defeat, and derail your story so that you never see the full impact God wants you to have in the world. That's why it is important to stay intentional and focused.

We also have short-term memories when it comes to the amazing work God has done in our lives. I remember watching the movie *Finding Nemo* with my daughters when they were little, and we would laugh at how Dory, the blue fish with the bad memory, could forget things so quickly. But having a short-term memory also seems to be part of our human nature. We often live out our relationship with God in exactly the same way—losing sight of the theme of our story because we don't remember all the miraculous work He has already done. This isn't a new development; it is the long-running story of the people of God: we too easily forget His faithfulness.

In the book of Exodus, the Israelites see God do some shock-and-awe miracles. He leads them through the nights with a pillar of fire, parts the Red Sea, and destroys the greatest army on earth. What do they do a few short days after? They forget all those miracles and complain to Moses that God has left them to starve in the wilderness! It sounds crazy, but we do the same thing in our own faith journey.

We need the story of the Bible to point us back to the theme and direction of our lives. We need the community of faith to remind us of God's love and grace. And we need prayer and time alone with God to remember how far we have come and where we are headed.

In *My Story, Your Glory* we are going to look at every corner of our lives, every chapter of our stories, and remember the ways that the God of the universe has faithfully provided, orchestrated, and navigated us on our journeys. Your story matters, and God wants to use every part of it for His Glory. The book of Revelation says that the enemy is overcome by the blood of the Lamb *and the word of our testimony*. That means your story is playing a part in the redemption of the world! I promise you there isn't a single part of your story that God doesn't plan for good.

Now is the perfect time to revisit the truth found in the story God is writing for you . . .

Are you in a chapter of confusion? Remembering God's faithfulness can shine a light of clarity on where He is taking you.

Are you living through a painful part of your story? God wants to remind you that He is with you and will use even this.

Are you lost right now and need to come back home? Well, God loves to write a great comeback story.

Are you worried about an unknown or uncertain future? He is inviting you to learn what it looks like to live a story of trust and surrender.

Are you in a blessed and joyful chapter? God wants you to live a story of gratitude.

What about the painful chapters in your past that you wish you could rip out of the book? The Author of your story sees every part and wants you to invite Him into even the broken chapters no one else sees.

Can't seem to make your story go the way you want it to? God wants to show you that His plan for you is the best plan.

Maybe you feel a million miles away from the story you thought your life was going to tell. God wants to write a beautiful new chapter of your life starting today.

The Bible says that we—the people of God—are His craftmanship. We are made in His image. This is the truest part of your story. You serve a God who loved you so much He gave His only Son so you would have everlasting life. He has invited you to play a role in the greatest story ever: the story of redemption and restoration of all of creation. As you open these pages, I hope you will be reminded that the author and perfector of our faith is intentional, right down to the smallest plot details, and that He wants to use it all for His Glory.

HOW TO USE THIS DEVOTIONAL

This devotional was designed to help you focus on the good news of your story as a follower of Jesus. Each day challenges you to consider a new truth of what God is currently doing or has done in your life. Each of the thirty days will challenge you to turn the focus of your life toward reflecting the glory of the One who loves you.

CONNECT to His Story includes a Bible study passage to help ground you in the truth of Scripture as well as questions for discussion with your small group (or further personal study).

Each **CRAFT Your Story** section is an opportunity for you to write and reflect on your own life and how God is working in your story. You can do this in a personal journal, in notes on your phone, or even at my ministry's website: popwe.org. The point of this activity is to build a journal record of your story with God.

The **SHARE Your Story** daily activity provides ideas for sharing God's work in your story with others in your community. We can lift one another up and encourage those around us to keep moving forward in our faith journey when we boldly share our testimonies of God's faithfulness. You can choose to do these activities in your own way, or you can post them on the website.

Finally, each *My Story* devotional day provides a challenge called **LIVE Your Story** that will help you to live out how God's glory manifests in your life, in your community, in your neighborhood. These ideas and activities are designed to help you put God's love into practice!

It is so important to pay attention to the direction God is taking our lives and to be intentional about remembering His faithfulness. When you complete this thirty-day devotional, you will have a journal that documents God's enduring presence—a written testimony that you can return to again and again for encouragement. My ministry, popwe (popwe.org), offers some powerful resources that can help you connect with others who are seeking God's glory in their story.

I pray this devotional becomes a tool you return to during difficult times or whenever you need a reminder of God's love, grace, and faithfulness. I'm excited to spend thirty days with you learning how to craft, share, and live a more meaningful and fulfilling story with the one life we get to live. It's your story for His Glory.

My Life Story, Your Glory

Ever since humans began using the written word, they have been working to find a way to cover up their mistakes. Did you know that once a upon a time people actually used moist bread to erase their writing errors? I don't know about you, but I can't imagine wasting something as delicious as a Panera bagel or an Olive Garden breadstick just to hide a misspelled word. Fortunately for all the bread lovers of the world, Edward Nairne developed and marketed the very first rubber eraser in 1770.

Nearly two hundred years later (in 1956), an American typist named Bette Nesmith Graham invented a correction fluid that we know today as Wite-Out. (As a music fan, I feel compelled to tell you she was also the mother of Mike Nesmith, one of the members of the

1960s pop band The Monkees!) Bette helped save the jobs of countless receptionists and made a ton of money doing it. As computers came along, the good old delete key provided us with a super easy way to get rid of our mistakes. Of course, if you use an Apple product now, you can even "unsend" messages on your iPhone and computer. This compulsion to erase what we have written extends into our lives too.

I know what many of you are thinking: *If only it were that easy to erase the unwanted sentences, paragraphs, and chapters of our own lives.* Unfortunately, no moist bread, eraser, Wite-Out, or delete key can undo the parts of our own story we don't like. We've all said and done things we wish we could undo. I have a few examples of my own, and by the time you read this I will have a few more. It is just part of being human.

But have you ever considered that maybe when we are tempted to hide those parts of our life, to white them out so that no one can see them—that isn't part of God's plan? What if instead of trying to *erase*, we simply handed our story over to God and trusted Him to *reclaim* and *redeem* our story by rewriting it in His own handwriting?

When we read about the apostle Paul's life and ministry, we find that he was not concerned at all about "whiting out" the parts of his past that he most regretted.

He didn't shy away from the bad parts of his story. Saul had terrorized and imprisoned the early Christians. He understood that God's grace is not some "magic eraser in the sky." God stepped into his life, changed his name, and began to retell his story. After his conversion, Paul was not only transparent about the mistakes of his past but was also honest about continuing to struggle with sin (Romans 7). God reframes our stories with words of love and retells our lives in the nurturing light of His redemptive plan.

God takes broken sentences and uses them to rewrite your life into something beautiful. I think that's why Paul acknowledged freely (and to all who would listen to him) that he was the *worst* of sinners. He was free to share the redemptive truth of his entire story—not just the shiny and glossy parts—because he understood that God was using every line to bring others closer to the truth of His love.

Today I want to challenge you to embrace the truth that God is aware of every line, every sentence, every paragraph, yes, every chapter of your story and He isn't scared off by any of it. God knows every detail, and He *still* loves you. In fact, He wants to step into the darkest and most broken parts and use that very material to build something beautiful. God doesn't even bother with a delete key—He is too busy rewriting.

CONNECT TO HIS STORY

Read the following passages and consider how they apply
to your life:

ACTS 8:1–3 *"And Saul approved of their killing him. On
that day a great persecution broke out against the church
in Jerusalem, and all except the apostles were scattered
throughout Judea and Samaria. Godly men buried Stephen
and mourned deeply for him. But Saul began to destroy the
church. Going from house to house, he dragged off both
men and women and put them in prison."*

ROMANS 7:22–23 *"For in my inner being I delight in God's
law; but I see another law at work in me, waging war against
the law of my mind and making me a prisoner of the law of
sin at work within me."*

1 TIMOTHY 1:15–16 *"Here is a trustworthy saying that
deserves full acceptance: Christ Jesus came into the world
to save sinners—of whom I am the worst. But for that very
reason I was shown mercy so that in me, the worst of sinners, Christ Jesus might display his immense patience as
an example for those who would believe in him and receive
eternal life."*

How do you think the early Christians felt about
Saul/Paul and his conversion?

How does Paul use his past as a testimony to God's grace? What are some of the ways that God rewrites Paul's story "line by line and word by word"?

What area of your life do you think God wants to use as a testimony to His redeeming love and grace?

CRAFT YOUR STORY

In your journal, take some time to document a part of your story that you have resisted handing over to God. Maybe it is a difficult season of your life or a time when you struggled spiritually or hurt others. Maybe it is that sentence you wish you wouldn't have spoken. Consider if you have hidden or tried to white it out rather than handing it over to Him. How might God want to rewrite that area of your life?

SHARE YOUR STORY

Write the names of three people who need to hear how God is rewriting your story. Maybe you know of someone hurt by that unwanted part of your story or someone struggling in a similar way who would be encouraged by God's work in your life. Plan to spend some time with these people in the next few weeks and share your testimony.

LIVE YOUR STORY

Find a quiet place today to spend some time in prayer and ask God to provide you with new words for that part of your story you are struggling with the most. Think about how God used Paul, the "worst of sinners," to bring others closer to Him. He wants to rewrite your life, line by line.

Write down three words that come to mind as you pray and read Scripture, then post those words someplace where you can see them every day as a reminder that the Author of all things is always adding His own words to your story.

NOTES

My Identity, Your Glory

I recently took my family on a vacation to New York City. When I think of the term *vacation*, I picture white sand beaches, sunshine, a book, and falling asleep in a beach chair while listening to the tide roll in and out. But when you're a girl dad, you learn that the word *vacation* is often interchangeable with the word *shopping*. And when it comes to shopping, New York City is the place to be.

We had a blast shopping our way through the Big Apple. But one evening we found ourselves smack-dab in the middle of a very crowded Times Square. We were quickly engulfed by a crowd of protesters, street entertainers, tourists, people selling watches and purses, and a host of interesting characters. The intensity of the scene made my protective instincts kick in. "Stay close," I said as I took my daughters by their hands and led them through the intimidating crowd. People were shouting slogans and selling their wares, and we were overwhelmed by the chaos around us. It would have been so easy for us to get separated, and I was not about to let go of my girls in the middle of that madness. As long as they stayed close to me, they could block out all the yelling, stay safe, and keep heading in the right direction.

That moment in the crowds of that big city sometimes feels like a metaphor for my spiritual life. It seems as if we are constantly being pulled in different directions by the shouts of our broken world and by our own sinful nature attempting to lead us astray. And when we lose touch with our heavenly Father, we can lose sight of who we are and be fooled into adopting an identity that the world wants to assign us, one far from the true identity given to us by a loving Creator:

> Your challenges in school can make you feel like your name is *Stupid*.
> A dysfunctional family situation can make you feel like your name is *Unwanted*.
> The mistakes you've made can make you believe your name is *Failure*.
> A spouse walks out, and you are left believing your name is *Worthless*.

I heard a preacher say once that we spend too much time playing "dress up" and putting on identities of the world rather than leaning into who God made us to be. It reminds me of a Henri Nouwen quote I came across: "Spiritual identity means we are not what we do or what people say about us. And we are not what we have. We are the beloved daughters and sons of God."

My role as a dad has helped me better understand the importance of staying close to my heavenly Father for direction, for assurance, for identity.

Like all those people shouting in Times Square, if we follow the leads and the voices of other people instead of God's, we soon lose the true story of who we are in Him. Satan knows that if he can get you and me to believe a lie about who we are, we'll never be able to step fully and freely into the plan that God has for us.

The Bible tells us the truth of our God-given identity: "See what great love the Father has lavished on us, that we should be called children of God! And that is what we are!" (1 John 3:1). A relationship with Christ also means your identity is found in Him no matter where you have been or what you have done. The God of the universe is only interested in the identity that He has given you.

We are God's handiwork, His craftsmanship. The psalmist reminds us that we were known by our Creator while we were still in the womb (Psalm 139:13). We are *known* by God! He knows us better than we know ourselves. It makes sense for us to look to Him when searching for our identity and place in this world. Just like my daughters needed to stay close to me in the middle of that noisy, wild New York City crowd, we must always stay close to our heavenly Father. If we focus on walking hand in hand with Him and hear His voice over the messages of this world, we will hear Him calling us by our true name—the only name that matters.

Remember that the journey to discover your true identity begins by staying close to your heavenly Father. Today, remind yourself that *you are who God says you are*, and you are living a story that gives Him all the glory.

CONNECT TO HIS STORY

Read the following passage and consider how it applies to your life:

EPHESIANS 1:3–10 *"Praise be to the God and Father of our Lord Jesus Christ, who has blessed us in the heavenly realms with every spiritual blessing in Christ. For he chose us in him before the creation of the world to be holy and blameless in his sight. In love he predestined us for adoption to sonship through Jesus Christ, in accordance with his pleasure and will—to the praise of his glorious grace, which he has freely given us in the One he loves. In him we have redemption through his blood, the forgiveness of sins, in accordance with the riches of God's grace that he lavished on us. With all wisdom and understanding, he made known to us the mystery of his will according to his good*

pleasure, which he purposed in Christ, to be put into effect
when the times reach their fulfillment—to bring unity to all
things in heaven and on earth under Christ."

Think about the words Paul uses in this passage to describe our relationship with Christ.

What is your identity as a believer according to this passage?

What are the riches of God's grace in your life? How can you share that with others?

CRAFT YOUR STORY

Spend a few moments today writing about your identity. How do you define yourself? How would you describe yourself to others? Now write about how God sees you. What is your identity in Him? Think about how you need to adjust your own view of your identity to coincide with your true identity in Christ.

SHARE YOUR STORY

Reach out to someone you know and encourage them that they are a son or daughter of God—that they can find their identity not in the things the world says but in Christ. Everyone is facing a battle for their identity, and today God could use you to be a much-needed reminder for someone else that they are a beloved child of God.

LIVE YOUR STORY

Spend some time researching what the Bible says about your identity in Christ. Pick out two or three verses to memorize and keep close to your heart in times when you are tempted to let the world define you.

NOTES

DAY 3

My Purpose, Your Glory

Early in my career my answer was always "yes" when I was asked to sing somewhere. It didn't matter where, how, or to whom, my response was always, "I'm in!" As you can imagine, this led me into many, shall we say, "interesting" experiences. I performed at youth groups, retirement homes, schools, birthdays, weddings, funerals, churches, and even a biker bar. One time, I was even booked to perform at a West Virginia school of mining (yes, you read that correctly). I wondered if my concert was going to be underground and considered the very real possibility that my audience would be wearing hard hats and have faces soiled by soot from the coal mines.

When I drove to West Virginia from Tennessee, I was surprised to find that the campus was a *complete* ghost town. I saw posters promoting my show on the walls of the student center, but there were no students anywhere. I wandered around for a half hour before I could finally track down a real human being. "I'm sorry, there must have been a scheduling mix-up," the guy explained. "This weekend is our fall break. All the students have gone home. But you are welcome to still play if you want to get paid." So I set up my gear, took out my guitar, and played my whole set to an empty room. And that night went down in the history books for me as my smallest audience ever at a show.

The truth is that I was humiliated that night in West Virginia. I finished my evening by soothing my sorrows with a Bloomin' Onion at the local Outback Steakhouse— right next to the Red Roof Inn where I would sleep before making the long drive back to Nashville. These days I'm thankful to see a couple more people attending my concerts than I had that night, but I can also find myself becoming fixated on the wrong things. How many people am I reaching? How many people came to my concert? How many people am I really impacting? Does the audience like me? Are they singing along with the new songs? Is my latest going to be a hit? The truth is that God is not concerned with that stuff. It turns out I learned a big lesson from that West Virginia concert for no one.

I realized how easy it can be to lose sight of *why* we are actually here. God's calling, our purpose, has nothing to do with the approval of an audience. No matter our line of work or our purpose in life, it is human nature to get overly concerned with pleasing the wrong people. The apostle Paul explains in Galatians 1:10, "Am I now trying to win the approval of human beings, or of God? Or am I trying to please people? If I were still trying to please people, I would not be a servant of Christ."

Paul says that pleasing the crowd isn't a story that gives God glory. The world always talks about "chasing a dream," but far more satisfying (and eternal) than a dream is pursuing God's calling for your life. We've all been uniquely designed with special gifts, talents, relationships, and responsibilities, and God has placed us here for a purpose. Whether you're a stay-at-home mom, a teacher, a garbage collector, or a college student, there is no heavenly hierarchy in God's kingdom. He's concerned about the *eternal* impact of your life, which is why He is the only audience who matters.

Looking back, as humiliating as it felt to be standing in that student center singing to an empty room, I see it differently now. In fact, these days as I step into a crowded church, a packed theater, or a standing-room-only arena, I often close my eyes and see myself back in that college singing my heart out to the one who made me and gives me purpose. I live my life for an audience of one. My only aim is to fulfill His calling on my life and let God take care of the rest. I may not see the results of my efforts, but as long as I've done what God has called me to do, then I can rest knowing that my purpose will somehow bring God glory.

I want to be like that servant in Matthew 25 who takes the Master's investment and faithfully multiplies it. I want to hear "well done" from the only one who matters. My story is for Him. My songs are for Him. Whether I hear the applause of man or the criticism of the crowd, it does not define me or decide if my story is successful.

Wherever you are in your story today, keep your eyes fixed on Him for your approval so that your purpose can bring Him glory.

CONNECT TO HIS STORY

Read the following passage and consider how it applies to your life:

> **MATTHEW 25:14–23** *"Again, it will be like a man going on a journey, who called his servants and entrusted his wealth to them. To one he gave five bags of gold, to another two bags, and to another one bag, each according to his ability. Then he went on his journey. The man who had received five bags of gold went at once and put his money to work and gained five bags more. So also, the one with two bags of gold gained two more. But the man who had received one bag went off, dug a hole in the ground and hid his master's money. After a long time, the master of those servants returned and settled accounts with them. The man who had received five*

bags of gold brought the other five. 'Master,' he said, 'you entrusted me with five bags of gold. See, I have gained five more.' His master replied, 'Well done, good and faithful servant! You have been faithful with a few things; I will put you in charge of many things. Come and share your master's happiness!' The man with two bags of gold also came. 'Master,' he said, 'you entrusted me with two bags of gold; see, I have gained two more.' His master replied, 'Well done, good and faithful servant! You have been faithful with a few things; I will put you in charge of many things. Come and share your master's happiness!'"

What does Jesus's parable say about His investment in you?

How can you be more faithful with what God has entrusted you with?

What are the "bags of gold" in your life—the talents, relationships, and responsibilities that God wants you to invest and multiply?

What does this passage teach us about focusing on pleasing God?

CRAFT YOUR STORY

Name an area in your life where God is calling you to turn your focus to Him. What is your purpose? Is it a talent? A relationship? A responsibility? Write about what it means for you to look to Him for approval in this area of your life.

SHARE YOUR STORY

Spend some time thinking about how it feels when you look only to God for approval rather than to everyone else. Write about a situation in your life where you have done that. What was the result? How can you encourage others to do the same? Share that instance with someone in your family, your small group, or your faith community today.

LIVE YOUR STORY

Choose an area of your life where you want to commit to God but struggle with focusing on the approval of others. Find a prayer partner and spend some time praying about this specific talent, relationship, or responsibility each day this week.

NOTES

My Service, Your Glory

Years ago, I wrote a song called "Do Something" that asked the question, "If not us, then who?" That song was about my tendency to look around at all the pain, injustices, hunger, homelessness, and a million other problems in our world and ask God to do something about it. The truth is that whenever I ask that question of God, His response in my heart (and as I read the Bible) is pretty convicting. It's as if He is saying, "I *did* do something. I created *you*."

Talk about a wake-up call! But with all the world's problems, where do you even begin? I think of James 1:22: "Do not merely listen to the word. . . . Do what it says." In other words, just do something.

Jesus explains in one of the most convicting moments in Scripture that we are here to care for one another and that the stakes are eternal. If we ignore the needs of the world, He will respond to us in the same way: "Depart from me, you who are cursed, into the eternal fire prepared for the devil and his angels. For I was hungry and you gave me nothing to eat, I was thirsty and you gave me nothing to drink, I was a stranger and you did not invite me in, I needed clothes and you did not clothe me, I was sick and in prison and you did not look after me" (Matthew 25:41–43).

Whenever I sing "Do Something" lately, it makes me think about my friend Tim Tebow. Every time I'm with him, whether it's backstage at a speaking event or in a conversation on my podcast, he never wants to talk about his Heisman Trophy, his two National Championships, his MVP award, his pro football career, or how many touchdowns he scored. Tim draws all his energy and passion from serving the kingdom of God by serving others. He lights up to share the great work the Tim Tebow Foundation is doing across the globe as they care for what Tim calls the "MVPs" (most vulnerable people). The thing I admire so much about Tim is that he doesn't wait around for someone else to do the work when he sees a need. He is a committed servant. He is stepping into action to find ways to care for others and carry the hope of Jesus to a broken and hurting world.

Have you ever spent time in the presence of someone who is living their story that loudly? I'm not talking about how loud they preach the gospel. I'm talking about how loud their *service* to others preaches the good news. When you're around someone like that who walks the walk and talks the talk, it inspires you to do the same.

I am motivated to serve when I'm around Tim Tebow. I am encouraged to serve others when I'm with Sissy Goff, who dedicates her life to counseling children. I am fired up to do something when I'm with my friend Diane in Colorado, who dedicates countless hours of her day as a board member of multiple nonprofit organizations, helping raise money for their valuable services. I am inspired by my wife, Emily, and the way that she rallies all of her friends to adopt families in need at Christmastime, providing gifts for children every year.

As followers of Jesus, we are called to serve those in need. We are called to be the hands and feet of the One who loves us so much that He died for our sins. And when I walk out my front door each day, I am supposed to keep my eyes open for Jesus. Scripture tells us that whenever we do anything for our neighbor or for the "least of these," we are serving Him.

I know that living my life for God's glory doesn't have to involve my vocal cords. Sure, what we say is important, but what we *do* changes other people's stories. Living my story for His Glory is about letting the life I live and my service to others speak. Following Jesus is about making the choice not to sit back and wait for someone else to do something when I see a need. I want to be able to say that I responded to Jesus's call in Matthew 25: "For I was hungry and you gave me something to eat, I was thirsty and you gave me something to drink, I was a stranger and you invited me in, I needed clothes and you clothed me, I was sick and you looked after me, I was in prison and you came to visit me."

How is God calling you to serve today? What are the needs you see in your family, church, and community? God is calling you to serve Him and play a part in the story of redemption He is writing in all of creation.

CONNECT TO HIS STORY

Read the following passage and consider how it applies to your life:

> **MATTHEW 25:31-46** *"When the Son of Man comes in his glory, and all the angels with him, he will sit on his glorious throne. All the nations will be gathered before him, and he will separate the people one from another as a shepherd separates the sheep from the goats. He will put the sheep on his right and the goats on his left. Then the King will say to those on his right, 'Come, you who are blessed by my Father; take your inheritance, the kingdom prepared for you since the creation of the world. For I was hungry and you gave me something to eat, I was thirsty and you gave me something to drink, I was a stranger and you invited me in, I needed*

clothes and you clothed me, I was sick and you looked after me, I was in prison and you came to visit me.' Then the righteous will answer him, 'Lord, when did we see you hungry and feed you, or thirsty and give you something to drink? When did we see you a stranger and invite you in, or needing clothes and clothe you? When did we see you sick or in prison and go to visit you?' The King will reply, 'Truly I tell you, whatever you did for one of the least of these brothers and sisters of mine, you did for me.' Then he will say to those on his left, 'Depart from me, you who are cursed, into the eternal fire prepared for the devil and his angels. For I was hungry and you gave me nothing to eat, I was thirsty and you gave me nothing to drink, I was a stranger and you did not invite me in, I needed clothes and you did not clothe me, I was sick and in prison and you did not look after me.' They also will answer, 'Lord, when did we see you hungry or thirsty or a stranger or needing clothes or sick or in prison, and did not help you?' He will reply, 'Truly I tell you, whatever you did not do for one of the least of these, you did not do for me.' Then they will go away to eternal punishment, but the righteous to eternal life."

CRAFT YOUR STORY

Write about the needs you have noticed in your family, neighborhood, or community. How can you better respond to those needs with service? Write about what

God might be calling you to do to help others right now and how you plan to respond.

SHARE YOUR STORY

Was there a time when you were in need and someone gave you help? How did that person reflect the love of Jesus into your life? How can you model that same giving spirit for others?

LIVE YOUR STORY

How can you inspire others to serve? This week take the time to organize a group of friends, your small group, people from your church, or some neighborhood friends and plan a service project to help others and spread the love of God in our hurting world.

NOTES

My Trust, Your Glory

My wife bought me a T-shirt once to wear as we celebrated the Fourth of July that read, "Fireworks Director: If I run, you run." I wore it proudly as I risked my life to light our family fireworks show that I'm quite sure was anything but safe.

The truth is, I have no qualifications that make me a *trustworthy* director of any sort of fireworks show. I've been known to burn myself just trying to start up a barbecue grill. I remember the minute I lit the fuse of the biggest firework I had purchased, I began sprinting away from the pending explosion. In my imagination, I looked like an action movie hero, narrowly escaping a fiery blast. But I'm guessing I looked more like a sweaty dad who had no clue what he was doing. Only a fool would blindly trust any so-called wisdom I may try to impart about the inner workings of a Roman candle.

Trust is a deeply important concept. We live with an incredible amount of trust just by getting on planes, taking Ubers and cabs, sending our kids to school each day. Yet the reality is that we also tend to put our trust in unworthy and unqualified sources of wisdom all the time. I scrolled through Instagram one morning and noticed this guy talking about how to turn $5,000 into $500,000 and all I had to do was just follow his advice. I recognized him: just months ago, he was marketing himself as an expert worship leader who could help you write the perfect song and hone your craft as a songwriter. Now, he's pivoted and become a "financial expert" ready to help you escape the middle class and build wealth.

If you google the word *trust*, you'll find thousands of articles about its importance. *Psychology Today* explains it as "a key element of social relationships and a foundation for cooperation. It is critical for romantic relationships, friendships, interactions between strangers, and social groups on a large scale, and a lack of trust in such scenarios can come with serious consequences. Indeed, society as a whole would likely fail to function in the absence of trust."*

* "Trust," *Psychology Today*, accessed December 13, 2023, https://www.psychologytoday.com/us/basics/trust.

So, the question is, Whom should you trust? Proverbs 3:5–6 urges us to "trust in the LORD with all your heart, and do not lean on your own understanding. In all your ways acknowledge him, and he will make straight your paths" (ESV). Scripture makes it clear that the Lord is the only one worthy of our complete trust.

There is a story in the Bible about a guy named Daniel who gets thrown into a lions' den simply for being a faithful servant—but his trust in God gets him through the night surrounded by hungry lions! That makes me think of how, in daily life, people might catch our attention with a flashy Instagram post, or we might unearth a positive takeaway in someone's advice. But we must look carefully at the source. In the lions' dens of life, we wouldn't lean on a fancy Instagram account with a blue check mark. We wouldn't hope that a motivational speaker could keep the mouths of the lions closed. We probably wouldn't bet on the latest popular self-help book to see us through the darkest night.

I don't know about you, but I'm trusting my story to the one and only miracle-working, grace-giving author and finisher of my faith. I am trusting the God who made me and loves me enough to lead me through life—even in the most hopeless situations. I am trusting the One who is who He says He is and always does what He promises He will do.

If we want our story to bring Him glory, we must begin by trusting Him. I love how author Brennan Manning explains it so beautifully in his book *Ruthless Trust*: "Trust is our gift back to God, and he finds it so enchanting that Jesus died for love of it."*

Let's be careful not to mistake the counterfeit voices vying for our trust for the real One who is worthy of it.

CONNECT TO HIS STORY

Read the following passage and consider how it applies to your life:

> **DANIEL 6:13-23** *"Then they answered and said before the king, 'Daniel, who is one of the exiles from Judah, pays no attention to you, O king, or the injunction you have signed, but makes his petition three times a day.' Then the king, when he heard these words, was much distressed and set his mind to deliver Daniel. And he labored till the sun went down to rescue him. Then these men came by agreement to the king and said to the king, 'Know, O king, that it is a law of the Medes and Persians that no injunction or ordinance that the king establishes can be changed.' Then the king commanded, and Daniel was brought and cast into the den of lions. The king declared to Daniel, 'May your God, whom*

* Brennan Manning, "Ruthless Trust: The Ragamuffin's Path to God," (HarperOne: 2000).

you serve continually, deliver you!' And a stone was brought and laid on the mouth of the den, and the king sealed it with his own signet and with the signet of his lords, that nothing might be changed concerning Daniel. Then the king went to his palace and spent the night fasting; no diversions were brought to him, and sleep fled from him. Then, at break of day, the king arose and went in haste to the den of lions. As he came near to the den where Daniel was, he cried out in a tone of anguish. The king declared to Daniel, 'O Daniel, servant of the living God, has your God, whom you serve continually, been able to deliver you from the lions?' Then Daniel said to the king, 'O king, live forever! My God sent his angel and shut the lions' mouths, and they have not harmed me, because I was found blameless before him; and also before you, O king, I have done no harm.' Then the king was exceedingly glad, and commanded that Daniel be taken up out of the den. So Daniel was taken up out of the den, and no kind of harm was found on him, because he had trusted in his God." (ESV)

What does the story of Daniel teach you about God's faithfulness in the direst situations?

What about the story of Daniel trusting God can help you with trust in your life, your relationships, your community?

Have you been faced with a "lions' den" situation where you had no one else to rely on but God?

CRAFT YOUR STORY

Write about a situation where you had to trust God. What did you learn from that experience about God? Explain what you learned about yourself.

SHARE YOUR STORY

List the reasons that you trust God. Share that list with a friend, accountability partner, small group, or someone you think needs to be encouraged to trust God.

LIVE YOUR STORY

What is one area of your life where you feel God is calling you to trust Him today? Spend some time in prayer over the next few days asking God to help you trust Him to write a better story in your life.

NOTES

DAY 6

My Courage, Your Glory

How often are we called on to be courageous? How many times are you required to be bold about your beliefs or stand up for those who can't stand on their own? How often do you really have to face down fear?

One of the first things I think about whenever I hear the word *courage* are the stories of the brave firefighters who charged into the burning towers at the World Trade Center on September 11. One of the great stories in the days after the towers collapsed was how many survivors talked about "a man in a red bandana" who had saved their lives. His name was Welles Remy Crowther—an equities trader and volunteer firefighter. Welles went up the stairs of the South Tower into the flames so others could come down safely. Because of his courage, there are eighteen people still alive today who would have perished in that terror attack.

Something about those firefighters, young and old, *choosing* to courageously charge up the stairwells of the burning towers points to the world-changing, sacrificial power that Jesus speaks of in John 15:13 when He says, "Greater love has no one than this: to lay down one's life for one's friends."

Those stories of courage also remind me of an Old Testament story in the book of Daniel, about three friends who stood before King Nebuchadnezzar and faced a terrifying fiery furnace. Shadrach, Meshach, and Abednego were brought before the king and questioned about why they wouldn't worship him. The law required anyone who disobeyed this command to be thrown into the fire. In a moment of incredible courage and faithfulness to God, they refused to bow, trusting that their God could deliver them from the furnace. "But even if he does not," they said, "we will not serve your gods" (Daniel 3:17–18).

These friends took the kind of stand that resonates across eternity. They stuck together and stayed faithful to God in the face of fear.

It's important to understand that courage doesn't mean the absence of fear. People who have shown great courage often talk about how they acted with boldness—even though they felt afraid. I believe that God helps us once we take those first courageous steps forward. Over and over again in the Bible, we see how God takes people's small, bold steps to write His greatest stories. Think of how scary it must have been for the Israelites to march into the Red Sea with the Egyptian army after them. Or in the book of Judges when God decided to cut Gideon's army from twenty-two thousand to ten thousand to three hundred men to go into battle with a large Midianite army. What about the courage of Peter in Acts to go before the high priest and declare the resurrected Jesus? Or when Paul decided to go bravely to Rome and preach the gospel? I think that God uses every bit of our courage—however small it seems—to write His story of redemption.

Today as you consider these incredible stories of courage, ask yourself where fear may be keeping you from the story God wants to write in your life. I wonder if God is just waiting for us to decide to be courageous in the way we love our neighbors, or in the way we stand up for our faith. Is He waiting for us to take a stand for the poor and the oppressed? What would it really look like to stand with courage in your family, your community, your work and boldly declare the love of Jesus? Are you to willing to run up the stairs? Be strong. Be courageous. Stand up for your faith in Him, and your story will be a story that reflects God's glory in a powerful way.

CONNECT TO HIS STORY

Read the following passage and consider how it applies to your life:

DANIEL 3:16-27 *"Shadrach, Meshach and Abednego replied to him, 'King Nebuchadnezzar, we do not need to defend ourselves before you in this matter. If we are thrown into the blazing furnace, the God we serve can deliver us from it, and he will deliver us from Your Majesty's hand. But even if he does not, we want you to know, Your Majesty, that we will not serve your gods or worship the image of gold you have set up.' Then Nebuchadnezzar was furious with Shadrach, Meshach and Abednego, and his attitude toward them changed. He ordered the furnace heated seven times hotter than usual and commanded some of the strongest soldiers in his army to tie up Shadrach, Meshach and Abed-nego and throw them into the blazing furnace. So these men, wearing their robes, trousers, turbans and other clothes, were bound and thrown into the blazing furnace. The king's command was so urgent and the furnace so hot that the flames of the fire killed the soldiers who took up Shadrach, Meshach and Abednego, and these three men, firmly tied, fell into the blazing furnace. Then King Nebu-chadnezzar leaped to his feet in amazement and asked his advisers, 'Weren't there three men that we tied up and threw into the fire?' They replied, 'Certainly, Your Majesty.' He said, "Look! I see four men walking around in the fire,*

> *unbound and unharmed, and the fourth looks like a son of*
> *the gods.' Nebuchadnezzar then approached the opening*
> *of the blazing furnace and shouted, 'Shadrach, Meshach*
> *and Abednego, servants of the Most High God, come out!*
> *Come here!' So Shadrach, Meshach and Abednego came*
> *out of the fire, and the satraps, prefects, governors and*
> *royal advisers crowded around them. They saw that the fire*
> *had not harmed their bodies, nor was a hair of their heads*
> *singed; their robes were not scorched, and there was no*
> *smell of fire on them."*

In this passage notice that Shadrach, Meshach, and Abednego tell the king they won't bow down even if God doesn't deliver them. What does that teach us about taking steps of courage in the face of uncertainty?

Why do you think the three friends speak with one voice in this passage?

Would the story of the friends be different if God had not rescued them from the fiery furnace?

What does this story say about God's response to our faithful courage?

How can we apply the truths of this passage to our daily life?

CRAFT YOUR STORY

Write about a situation where you had to show courage. Explain what happened and why. Consider the ways that

God was faithful to you in your steps of courage and write them down so that you will remember them next time you are faced with fear.

SHARE YOUR STORY

Think of an area in your life of faith where you struggle with fear. Share that with an accountability partner, your small group, your spouse, or even a pastor and commit to pray for courage in that area of your life.

LIVE YOUR STORY

Find someone to boldly share the love of God with today. Buy someone a cup of coffee, help someone who needs it, make a courageous move in the name of the love of Jesus today and see what He does with your story!

NOTES

My Shame, Your Glory

I have a friend who serves in prison ministry. He told me one of the first things he tries to do when he stands up in front of a group of inmates behind bars is to level the playing field. There can be no "holier than thou" attitude in an environment where a lot of guys are still dealing with the shame of their mistakes. He told me his favorite icebreaker joke that *always* makes the inmates laugh: "Hey guys, I want to start off by saying I'm just like all of you. Matter of fact, the only difference between me and you is that *you* got caught!"

It's his way of being transparent about his own imperfections and reminding his audience that we all make mistakes. We all have parts of our lives we are ashamed of and are tempted to hide.

One of the most quintessential Nashville music experiences is called a writer's round. On any given night, in live music venues all around my hometown, you can see songwriters sitting in a row on stage taking turns playing the songs they wrote. It is always a special experience because you just never know when you'll hear a big hit sung by the person behind the scenes who wrote it. A couple of years ago a few of my friends decided to turn this writer's round concept upside down. They asked the participants *not* to play any of their hit songs. Instead, they had to perform the absolute *worst* songs they had ever written. As you might imagine, this made for one hilarious evening—listening to one terrible song after another. But these writers were celebrating the truth that the same pen that wrote a big hit was just as capable of writing a bad song. They were celebrating that the shame of a bad song didn't get in the way of them writing a great song.

I think that the devil uses the shame of our mistakes to keep us from letting God write great songs into our lives. Shame is one of the devil's primary weapons. Remember that Adam and Eve hid in shame, and Peter tried to hide after he had denied Christ. We have a tendency as humans to cower in shame when God calls us to do the opposite.

The famous shame researcher Brené Brown explains that "shame is that warm feeling that washes over us, making us feel small, flawed, and never good enough."* But God didn't redeem you to feel small or not good enough. I know from experience: shame can try to convince you that you are disqualified from doing God's work of serving and loving others.

We've all got our own bad songs. What could it look like to no longer feel the need to hide those from the world? My fellow songwriters weren't embarrassed by their worst songs because they are known for so many incredible lyrics. The inmates who attend my friend's services become free when they can laugh and realize they are not much different from their pastor—God has reclaimed their story. We are free to acknowledge our brokenness, our bad ideas, and our mistakes in the light of God's love—we don't have to hide in shame.

God's love allows us to view our humble beginnings, our wrong turns, our bad ideas, our mistakes, and missteps in the light of His grace and forgiveness. This leads us to have the same desire Paul did—to view *all* parts of his story as essential to his message. He didn't downplay his worst chapters. He loved to tell who he was *before* God changed his life because, through that, God's glory was on full display. Don't let the enemy use shame as a weapon to discourage you from all that God is calling you to do.

---

* Brené Brown, *The Gifts of Imperfection: 10th Anniversary Edition* (Center City, MN: Hazelden Publishing, 2020), 52.

CONNECT TO HIS STORY

Read the following passage and consider how it applies to your life:

> **ACTS 26:8-16** *"Why should any of you consider it incredible that God raises the dead? I too was convinced that I ought to do all that was possible to oppose the name of Jesus of Nazareth. And that is just what I did in Jerusalem. On the authority of the chief priests I put many of the Lord's people in prison, and when they were put to death, I cast my vote against them. Many a time I went from one synagogue to another to have them punished, and I tried to force them to blaspheme. I was so obsessed with persecuting them that I even hunted them down in foreign cities. On one of these journeys, I was going to Damascus with the authority and commission of the chief priests. About noon, King Agrippa, as I was on the road, I saw a light from heaven, brighter than the sun, blazing around me and my companions. We all fell to the ground, and I heard a voice saying to me in Aramaic, 'Saul, Saul, why do you persecute me? It is hard for you to kick against the goads.' Then I asked, 'Who are you, Lord?' 'I am Jesus, whom you are persecuting,' the Lord replied. 'Now get up and stand on your feet.'"*

How is Paul using his own story in this passage to convince others about the truth of Jesus?

Does Paul seem to be dealing with the shame of his own history and background in this passage?

As you read about Paul's disbelief and his eagerness to persecute and disprove Christians before his conversion, what comes to mind in your own life and own past?

CRAFT YOUR STORY

In your journal, take some time to consider a part of your story that you tend to hide from other people. How has shame affected your ability to connect with other believers and do the work God is calling you to do?

SHARE YOUR STORY

Write about an area of your life that has caused you to hide in shame. Is it something that you need to share with someone you trust? Is it something you need to bring to God in prayer? Begin by spending time talking with God about it.

LIVE YOUR STORY

The enemy uses shame to keep us from experiencing the life God has for us. Today make a list of the things God is calling you to do or the people in your family, your faith community, or your neighborhood that He is calling you to minister to. Now walk in the light of how much God loves and *frees* you to do His work—not only will you have life and joy, but His power will be on display for others to see.

NOTES

My Thoughts, Your Glory

How often do you really think about what you think about? I know that may sound like a confusing riddle. According to Dr. Fred Luskin at Stanford University it is estimated that the average human has about sixty thousand thoughts per day.* That is a lot of thinking! So it isn't any wonder that the Bible focuses on the importance of the mind when it comes to our relationship with Christ. If you observe what you are thinking, you will quickly realize that your thoughts impact how you feel. And, of course, how you feel impacts what you do. And what you do impacts the story you are writing with your life (and the story God wants to write). It makes sense

---

* Dr. Fred Luskin, "A Thought is a Thought," Your Time to Grow, https://yourtimetogrow.com/a-thought-is-a-thought/.

that the enemy would try to wage war on our minds. He's got sixty thousand chances to trip us up every day!

The apostle Paul promises that we "have the mind of Christ" (1 Corinthians 2:16), but sometimes that feels like it just can't be true. I mean, let's be honest for a moment: How would you feel if all of the sixty thousand thoughts you had today were sent like text messages to all of the contacts in your phone? Just the idea of people hearing your every thought reminds me of a *Saturday Night Live* character in the '80s played by Kevin Nealon called "Mr. No Depth Perception," who had all kinds of problems. But his funniest was when he yelled out his uncomfortable opinions about his houseguests around the dinner table because he believed they couldn't hear him. His guests were shocked by the thoughts that he thought they couldn't hear!

Can you imagine if your every thought were announced at a dinner party? Thank goodness that isn't reality. But the nature of our thoughts really can impact our life. If every thought for today were compiled for you in a list that you could read, what would your list look like? Would it be full of negativity, worry, anger, lust, jealously, doubt, and bitterness?

Of course, it's impossible to control the thoughts that pop into our minds throughout the day, but the apostle Paul explains that we *can* control what we do with them and can influence the nature of those thoughts. In 2

Corinthians 10:5 we read how important it is to take *every* thought captive. In other words, while we can't always control the thoughts that come through our minds, we can make the decision not to let those thoughts control us. We can challenge each thought and hold it up to God's honest light, ask Him if it's from Him. Is it lovely? Is it pure? Is it true? If the answer is no, then we know that thought is one to be discarded, not acted on.

Paul then explains in Philippians that it truly matters what we allow our minds to consume. This reminds me of the old saying, "garbage in, garbage out." Often, our thoughts are informed and fed by the choices we make of what to watch, read, or listen to. Paul urges us to focus on "whatever is true, whatever is noble, whatever is right, whatever is pure, whatever is lovely, whatever is admirable—if anything is excellent or praiseworthy" (Philippians 4:8). I often have to challenge myself to focus on Him more and the voices in the world around me less.

Of course, this is all impossible to do without help. And God knows that we need His help. The Bible tells us that He has provided us a helper and a way forward in every circumstance we face. We have a helper in the Holy Spirit who can renew our minds and guide us toward the truth of His Word. I may get discouraged or even embarrassed by the random thoughts that pop into my head. But these moments make me run to Jesus. They remind me to spend time reading my Bible and meditating on Scripture.

We have to be willing to ask ourselves some tough questions: *Am I spending more time talking to Jesus or listening to a useless podcast? Am I doom-scrolling through Instagram for hours or reading the negative comments on X right before bed, or am I spending those precious moments thanking God for the blessings of my day? Is my focus on Him?*

I want to be conscious of what goes into my heart and mind. I want to rely on the Holy Spirit to navigate my way through those sixty thousand thoughts a day. A story that gives God glory is a life that strives to be like Jesus—even in our thoughts.

CONNECT TO HIS STORY

Read the following passage and consider how it applies to your life:

PHILIPPIANS 4:4-9 *"Rejoice in the Lord always. I will say it again: Rejoice! Let your gentleness be evident to all. The Lord is near. Do not be anxious about anything, but in every situation, by prayer and petition, with thanksgiving, present your requests to God. And the peace of God, which transcends all understanding, will guard your hearts and your minds in Christ Jesus. Finally, brothers and sisters, whatever is true, whatever is noble, whatever is right, whatever* *is pure, whatever is lovely, whatever is admirable—if any-thing is excellent or praiseworthy—think about such things. Whatever you have learned or received or heard from me, or seen in me—put it into practice. And the God of peace will be with you."*

In this passage, what are the ways Paul says you should focus your thoughts?

How might you put Paul's directions into practice in your daily life?

What is encouraging about Paul's instruction?

CRAFT YOUR STORY

Spend some time making a list of your thoughts. (Maybe you can keep them on a notes application on your phone or in a journal.) At the end of your day, read through the list. Do they reflect the spirit of Christ? Write about your thoughts and how they might affect the story that God wants to write in your life.

SHARE YOUR STORY

How has focusing your mind on Scripture, prayer, and praise shaped your thoughts? Take some time today to share your testimony with someone in your life.

LIVE YOUR STORY

As you go throughout your week, try to focus on capturing your thoughts and returning them to Christ. If you find yourself harboring thoughts of negativity, worry, anger, jealousy, or bitterness, take a moment to recognize them and say a prayer for renewal. Each time you do this you are taking a step toward the story God has for you.

NOTES

My Dependence, Your Glory

Sometimes I think that God's best work starts when you realize that you can't make it without His grace. We all get to that moment in our lives when we know our dependence on Him to make it through. And yet we are all tempted from time to time to take the pen out of God's hands and try to write our own stories rather than relying on Him. Somehow, we constantly forget that He is a much better storyteller than we are. Pride truly does come before a fall. Deep down, we all are aware of our own struggles and weaknesses because we have to face them every single day. I think all of our closest relationships are built on grace. My family would remind you that I am far from a perfect husband and dad. I get impatient, sometimes I get distracted, sometimes I lose sight of what's important. I don't know if I have a

day where I don't want a do-over in some area of my life,
work, ministry, relationships. Fortunately, God offers me
that kind of grace.

It gives me so much hope to read the stories of even
the "heroes" of the Bible. In their own way, they all came
face-to-face with how much they needed God's grace
and mercy in their stories. The apostle Paul was very
transparent with his faith community about his struggles with sin. King David didn't just commit adultery;
he also murdered Bathsheba's husband. Yet he became
Israel's greatest king—a man "after God's own heart."
Moses killed an Egyptian soldier and ran and had nothing but excuses when God called him into service, but
God used him to deliver Israel from slavery. Jonah ran
from God and hid under a tree until that little situation with the whale, and *then* he became a prophet of
God. And then there is Simon Peter. The guy whose
name literally means "the rock," but his behavior was
anything but solid. I mean, you want to talk about a guy
who needed a do-over . . . Peter denies he even knows
his dear friend and teacher Jesus not once, not twice, but
three times. He does this after he had sworn to Jesus that
he wouldn't! You know how you hope your real friends
would be there for you when times are tough? Peter's
denials all happened while Jesus was being beaten, spit
on, laughed at, and crucified. But Jesus didn't hesitate to

give Peter a second chance—"feed my sheep," Jesus told him—and Peter truly became part of the foundation of the early church. Peter understood his dependence on Jesus in Acts 4 as he testified to the resurrection before the very religious leaders who had sent his Lord and Savior to the cross. When we embrace the grace and mercy of God's second chances each day, we are free to pursue the life He has called us into. We have to learn to depend on Him!

Lamentations 3:22–23 speaks to me because it promises a constant stream of God's mercy . . . and the closer I get to God, the more I see how much I need that in my life. Why is it necessary that God's mercy is new every morning? Because we need it every day. I don't know about you, but I've tried to live the perfect day—and for over forty years I have found it to be impossible. I can't go one minute without *Him*. I am thankful we serve a God who walks closely with us and allows do-overs. We don't need to walk in fear of making mistakes. We don't need to live a life of anxiety and shame over our imperfections. We don't need to hang our head when we mess up. His mercy and grace are available every second of every day. We only need to depend on His great faithfulness. God is always ready to extend His compassionate second chances to us . . . always.

CONNECT TO HIS STORY

Read the following passages and consider how they apply to your life:

LUKE 22:54-62 *"Then seizing him, they led him away and took him into the house of the high priest. Peter followed at a distance. And when some there had kindled a fire in the middle of the courtyard and had sat down together, Peter sat down with them. A servant girl saw him seated there in the firelight. She looked closely at him and said, 'This man was with him.' But he denied it. 'Woman, I don't know him,' he said. A little later someone else saw him and said, 'You also are one of them.' 'Man, I am not!' Peter replied. About an hour later another asserted, 'Certainly this fellow was with him, for he is a Galilean.' Peter replied, 'Man, I don't know what you're talking about!' Just as he was speaking, the rooster crowed. The Lord turned and looked straight at Peter. Then Peter remembered the word the Lord had spoken to him: 'Before the rooster crows today, you will disown me three times.' And he went outside and wept bitterly."*

LAMENTATIONS 3:22-23 *"Because of the Lord's great love we are not consumed, for his compassions never fail. They are new every morning; great is your faithfulness."*

How did Peter feel in the moment that Jesus looked at him? What do you think led to Peter denying Jesus?

How do you think it empowered Peter to go through this experience and yet be embraced by Jesus after His resurrection?

How does the truth of God's character in Lamentations reflect what we know about Jesus's love for Peter?

Why does the writer of Lamentations use the phrase "new every morning"? How can our awareness of God's faithful compassion change the way we live our lives?

CRAFT YOUR STORY

Write about an experience from the past year where you wished you had a do-over. How did you handle that situation? Did you experience shame and guilt? Did you ask for forgiveness? In light of today's devotional about God's mercy and grace, write about how He views that do-over moment in your story.

SHARE YOUR STORY

We need fellow believers to remind us of God's grace and mercy. Take some time today to share with someone in your family, your small group, or your faith community about how God's grace and mercy is impacting your life.

LIVE YOUR STORY

Spend a few minutes today writing down your do-over moments from yesterday. Maybe it is something big such as losing your temper or small such as a work-related mistake, or even a relationship moment that may seem silly. Fold the list and set it somewhere where you can find it first thing in the morning. When you wake up tomorrow reread Lamentations 3:22–23, tear up the list, and throw it away as a reminder that God offers us that kind of mercy each new morning.

NOTES

My Praise, Your Glory

Growing up as a preacher's kid, I spent every Sunday morning in the front row of the church next to my mom and my brothers. As a result, church was the place where I felt as if the entire congregation was watching my every move. When you feel like all eyes are on you, the focus can become more about performance than praise. I remember having thoughts such as, *I should probably raise my hand during the slow song so the people behind me see that I'm the good preacher's son.* I didn't often get the chance to feel like worship was just between me and God. As I got older and began to lead worship, I realized that worship at its most important level is about taking your focus away from yourself and turning it to God. The heart of worship is praise, not performance.

A friend of mine talks about the importance of the "eye level" of your faith. He says you need to pay attention to where you keep your focus. I think about this sometimes when I am out on a run in my Tennessee neighborhood. If I look down at my feet, I can get caught up with how far I have to go; but if I look up, I tend to notice the rolling hills, the fall leaves, and the beauty all around me, and it propels me forward.

I don't know about you, but I get caught up "looking at my feet" throughout my day—whether it's an upcoming meeting, my long to-do list, or the next depressing news story on my phone. But when I raise my eyes up and look toward God, that action transforms my perspective. My friend says that beginning each day by praising God can help us fix our attention on the One who truly matters. When our eyes are on Him, we begin to notice His handiwork all around us. I've learned to start each morning with praise.

I remember the verses of the old hymn I used to sing in church: "to God be the glory, great things he has done." They remind me of how we can turn our whole lives around by praising God. Even when things aren't going well, praise can take your focus off your situation and place it on the One who can do great things. Just think of Acts 16 when Paul and Silas are imprisoned. Things don't look good, but what do they choose to do? They praise God. Then the prison doors are opened and they are miraculously freed.

In 2 Chronicles 20 we read of great armies marching against Israel. The situation seems bleak. What does the king choose to do? Praise God. Jehoshaphat praises God for the many miracles He has performed. In the midst of great trouble Israel responds by praising and worshipping God. Not exactly what you think they would do to prepare for advancing armies!

Praise is not confined to the worship songs we sing during a church service. And God has taught me that praise and worship actually transform the condition of my heart. When I praise Him for all He is doing in my life and in my community, it completely changes my outlook on the world.

Instead of beginning my prayer time by reading my long list of requests to God, I have discovered a radical shift in my focus when I begin with adoration, simply praising God for who He is, not for what I hope He will do for me. And I've noticed that the Psalms are centered on praise for God. As I meet Christians who have been walking with God for a long time and are mature in their faith, I find that they spend more time praising God than anything else. If you think about it, we were made to worship. So the essence of a story that gives God glory is one that lifts a sincere song of praise from the heart each and every day in each and every circumstance.

I'm learning to turn away from the distractions that keep my eyes looking down. I've freed myself from the pressure of performance when it comes to praise by keeping my eyes on Him. Because when we turn ourselves toward God in praise—when we focus on His Glory—that step lifts us up and propels us into the miraculous story He is writing in the world.

CONNECT TO HIS STORY

Read the following passage and consider how it applies to your life:

2 CHRONICLES 20:2-9 *"Some people came and told Jehoshaphat, 'A vast army is coming against you from Edom, from the other side of the Dead Sea. It is already in Hazezon Tamar' (that is, En Gedi). Alarmed, Jehoshaphat resolved to inquire of the LORD, and he proclaimed a fast for all Judah. The people of Judah came together to seek help from the LORD; indeed, they came from every town in Judah to seek him. Then Jehoshaphat stood up in the assembly of Judah and Jerusalem at the temple of the LORD in the front of the new courtyard and said: 'LORD, the God of our ancestors, are you not the God who is in heaven? You rule over all the kingdoms of the nations. Power and might are in your hand, and no one can withstand you. Our God, did you not drive out the inhabitants of this land before your people Israel and give it forever to the descendants of Abraham your friend? They have lived in it and have built in it a sanctuary for your Name, saying, "If calamity comes upon us,*

whether the sword of judgment, or plague or famine, we will
stand in your presence before this temple that bears your
Name and will cry out to you in our distress, and you will
hear us and save us."

Consider what you would do if you were Jehoshaphat in this situation. Can you think of a time when you felt like the odds were against you?

What does it take to spend time in praise in this kind of dire situation?

What does this Scripture say to you about the importance of praise and worship?

Read the rest of 2 Chronicles 20 to see how God responds to this situation. What does that say about the faithfulness of Jehoshaphat?

CRAFT YOUR STORY

Write about all the reasons you have to praise God right now (no matter your current situation). Write a list of praises to God and read those to Him today.

SHARE YOUR STORY

Find someone in your life—a prayer or accountability partner or a good friend—and spend a few moments sharing your list of reasons to praise God.

LIVE YOUR STORY

Make a commitment to spend some time in praise today—whether at the beginning of your prayer time or even while driving in your car. Sing His praises. Focus on how glorious God is today. Praise Him for being the author of your story. Focus your eyes on Him.

NOTES

DAY 11

My Patience, Your Glory

Sometimes it feels as if our life stories are stuck in a season that's just taking too long to tell. Maybe you feel caught in a difficult chapter and ready to turn the page. A job search that has dragged on for weeks, a health battle that keeps you in and out of doctors' offices and hospitals for months on end, or a family conflict that you've prayed about and still haven't seen the breakthrough. Maybe it's about waiting on the "right" person to come along, a financial miracle, or for God to provide you with clarity for a big decision. Whatever the situation, a season of waiting can be *so* difficult, especially when we can't see where God is going with our story.

I went through a difficult situation recently that seemed never-ending. Some days it felt as if my story was unfolding like the pace of Nashville's rush-hour traffic. No matter how much I prayed or how much I hoped, time dragged on slowly (for three long, difficult years). I was stuck on a page that just wouldn't turn and more than ready for a new chapter to begin. But during those moments of frustration when there was no break-through in sight, God also showed me that I was in very good company.

When you open the pages of the Bible, you begin to realize that waiting is part of the human experience. You also see what God can do with our patience. The Isra-elites waited and wandered through the wilderness for forty years before ever seeing the promised land. Think about the incredible story of Joseph, who, after being sold as a slave by his brothers, waited a *long* time before God placed him in a position of power. Noah waited on the Lord for over one hundred years building the ark and then had to wait patiently on God for dry land to appear after the Flood. And Abraham was told by God that he was to be the "father of many nations." Yet not until he was one hundred and his wife, Sarah, had passed ninety years old did they see God's promise of their son, Isaac, fulfilled. I was encouraged to find that there are just so many examples in Scripture of people who didn't see their miracle, their answer, their breakthrough overnight.

Our hope can be strengthened by reading these sto-ries of people who trusted God during the seemingly never-ending parts of their stories. Our faith can be restored as we read about God's faithfulness and how He comes through in His perfect timing—instead of ours. As a Christ follower, we are not just waiting; we are waiting on the Lord. Our hope is in a God who sees us, knows us, and has plans for us. And here's what the Bible promises will happen when we wait on the Lord: "But they who wait for the LORD shall renew their strength; they shall mount up with wings like eagles; they shall run and not be weary; they shall walk and not faint" (Isaiah 40:31, ESV).

Waiting on the Lord can be difficult. But I have learned over and over in my journey that while waiting isn't always fun, it always cultivates good things in my faith such as perseverance, endurance, and, yes, *patience*.

Here is the reality of the story that God is writing in your life: you don't know the next chapter, but He sure does. The Bible promises that the breakthrough is coming. God is working in ways we cannot see during seasons where we have to lean on our patience and hope in Him. I want to challenge you to never mistake your waiting for His absence. He is with you, and He is working. Wait on Him. Learn the practice of patience and watch His Glory unfold. When you choose to wait on the Lord instead of pushing through with your own strength to force a desired outcome, those around you will see whom you put your trust in. God's glory is on full display, even as you wait. The chapter of your life that feels never-ending is often the Master Storyteller just crafting something beautiful in your life. So lean into your patience and wait for His Glory.

CONNECT TO HIS STORY

Read the following passages and consider how they apply to your life:

> **GENESIS 18:1-2, 9-14** *"The LORD appeared to Abraham near the great trees of Mamre while he was sitting at the entrance to his tent in the heat of the day. Abraham looked up and saw three men standing nearby. When he saw them, he hurried from the entrance of his tent to meet them and bowed low to the ground.... 'Where is your wife Sarah?' they asked him. 'There, in the tent,' he said. Then one of them said, 'I will surely return to you about this time next year, and Sarah your wife will have a son.' Now Sarah was listening at the entrance to the tent, which was behind him. Abraham and Sarah were already very old, and Sarah was past the age of childbearing. So Sarah laughed to herself as she thought, 'After I am worn out and my lord is old, will I now have this pleasure?' Then the LORD said to Abraham, 'Why did Sarah laugh and say, "Will I really have a child, now that I am old?" Is anything too hard for the LORD? I will return to you at the appointed time next year, and Sarah will have a son.'"*

As you read this passage, what does it bring to mind in your own life?

Do you ever feel discouraged by your season of waiting like Sarah did? What are some ways that you can deal with these emotions?

This is likely not how Abraham imagined his story would unfold when God promised him that he would be the "father of nations." What does this teach you about waiting on God?

CRAFT YOUR STORY

Write about a season of waiting on God in your life. What did you learn during that time? How did God turn the page into the next chapter of life?

SHARE YOUR STORY

Write a note to someone who you know is waiting on God right now—whether it's for a medical, financial, or relational need—and encourage them that God is not finished with their story yet.

LIVE YOUR STORY

Today write down three areas of your life that are in "seasons of waiting." Spend some time in prayer this week asking God to give you patience in those areas as He writes the next chapter of your story.

NOTES

My Giving, Your Glory

Growing up in my dad's church, I remember a single mom named Barb. She was an avid tither who kept a notebook with three columns: one tracked her giving, the next she used to make a list of things she needed, and in the last column she recorded all the blessings that God gave to her. If she needed a new sofa, she would price it and then add it to her needs list. When God provided an almost-new sofa at half the price, she would credit "God's" column with the full amount the sofa would have cost her. At the end of the year, she would tally each column and excitedly report that God had outgiven her once again!

Barb was also such a cheerful giver. In her notebook she recorded the proof of all that God had done for her, and she never hesitated to give with abandon even though her needs were great. She understood the importance of remembering the blessings of the Lord and being thankful.

I learned from Barb's story that we can trust God to meet our needs. In fact, He will go above and beyond in His generosity back to us. I am not saying that when you give to God, He will make you rich. But Scripture does promise that God cares for us when we are generous with others. Philippians 4:19 reminds us that "this same God who takes care of me will supply all your needs from his glorious riches, which have been given to us in Christ Jesus" (NLT).

I often hear people say that they don't have much to give, but in one specific story, Jesus taught the importance of the *intention* of our generosity. As he watched a poor widow give all she had in the offering plate, He said to His disciples, "Truly I tell you, this poor widow has put more into the treasury than all the others. They all gave out of their wealth; but she, out of her poverty, put in everything—all she had to live on" (Mark 12:43–44).

And in all four Gospels, we see how Jesus demonstrated what God can do with the smallest offering—when He took five loaves and two fish and fed five thousand hungry people. In Jesus's day, having a daily meal was not always a guarantee. His miracle of feeding so many with so little reminds us that God can take what we may see as small and use it to meet the needs of many.

I want to match God's generosity in the way I live my life and give to others, and I want giving to be my default. I hope to raise my kids to understand that we are reflecting the love of Jesus to the world when we are generous. It is important to give with a joyful heart and a great attitude like my friend Barb did.

In one of my favorite TV commercials, the GEICO "Alligator Arms" demonstrates how human nature doesn't always lean into generosity. Can you picture the scene? A group of coworkers has just finished dinner when the check arrives. The alligator struggles with his short arms to take the check before he conveniently concludes, "I can't reach it." The commercial ends with the voice-over saying something like, "If you have alligator arms, you avoid picking up the check. It's what you do." It makes me laugh every time, but it also reminds me that God calls us to be better than the norm. He calls us to a *sacrificial* life of giving. I want my story to reflect God's generosity toward me.

I think the best parts of our story begin when we give faithfully—even the smallest amount. God likes to take our generosity and multiply it for the sake of others in the world. He is always looking to use our offerings to write His story into the hearts of our family, our neighbors, and our communities. So let's give with open hearts and joy so that our story can bring glory to Him.

CONNECT TO HIS STORY

Read the following passage and consider how it applies to your life:

> **JOHN 6:5–13** *"When Jesus looked up and saw a great crowd coming toward him, he said to Philip, 'Where shall we buy bread for these people to eat?' He asked this only to test him, for he already had in mind what he was going to do. Philip answered him, 'It would take more than half a year's wages to buy enough bread for each one to have a bite!' Another of his disciples, Andrew, Simon Peter's brother, spoke up, 'Here is a boy with five small barley loaves and two small fish, but how far will they go among so many?' Jesus said, 'Have the people sit down.' There was plenty of grass in that place, and they sat down (about five thousand men were there). Jesus then took the loaves, gave thanks, and distributed to those who were seated as much as they wanted. He did the same with the fish. When they had all had enough to eat, he said to his disciples, 'Gather the pieces that are left over. Let nothing be wasted." So, they gathered them and filled twelve baskets with the pieces of the five barley loaves left over by those who had eaten."*

How often do you relate to Philip in this passage and his worry about scarcity?

What does this story teach you about the way God cares for us?

Jesus takes what is available and does the miraculous to care for the needs of the people there. How can you apply this story to your own life today? What does it teach you about generosity toward your community and neighborhood?

CRAFT YOUR STORY

Write about a time in your life when you felt someone was generous with you. What was the situation? How did it help you? How did it make you feel about this person? Consider the ways this generous act reflects God's generosity with you.

SHARE YOUR STORY

Make a list of the ways that God has been generous in your life and share it with someone who may need that kind of encouragement today.

LIVE YOUR STORY

Spend some time coming up with practical ways you might live a more generous life. Maybe through giving at church or to a nonprofit? Maybe by being generous with someone in need—whether with time or resources? Pick three ways and follow through on them this week.

NOTES

My Forgiveness, Your Glory

I heard a story about a young man who carried a seventy-five-pound rock up a mountain as a fitness challenge. As if walking uphill isn't hard enough, think about how hard it would be carrying a rock that size. When he was finished, his hands were torn up and he was too exhausted to enjoy the view. Lately, I've noticed a trend that many people interested in fitness are wearing weighted vests when hiking at the park near my house. I guess carrying extra weight is supposed to do something good for your body, but most of the time I am content just walking or running in the Nashville summer without any extra weight to make it more difficult.

Years ago, I wrote a song called "Forgiveness," and I am pretty sure it holds the record for the longest it's *ever* taken me to complete a song. Seriously, it took me two years from start to finish. Why? Because every time I sat down to write about the importance of letting go of grudges and loving the unlovable, I felt like the biggest hypocrite on the planet. Honestly, I have a hard enough time forgiving a bad driver who cuts me off in rush-hour traffic, let alone someone who has deeply offended or hurt me. In the end, I discovered the only honest way I could write this song was to write it in the form of a prayer. Instead of saying, "Hey everybody, make sure you forgive those who hurt you," the most honest posture was to ask the Lord to help me let go of grudges and be a forgiving person. Because I knew I can't do it on my own.

Even as I write this book, I am keenly aware of relationships in my life that have not mended in the way I hoped they would have. Perhaps you can think of one or more of your own relationships currently in a fractured state. Jesus tells us to make sure we have forgiven others before we come to Him in prayer; He says we should forgive so that our heavenly Father can forgive us (Mark 11:25). The apostle Paul says we shouldn't let the sun go down on our anger (Ephesians 4:26–27).

I think there is a heaviness you carry when you don't forgive others. It is as if you are running the race of life while wearing a weighted vest. God wants us to run our race lighter and freer. I wonder how many people hold on to hurtful emotional weight in their life for way too long—kind of like carrying a seventy-five-pound rock up a mountain.

It's funny, my wife and I have disagreements, for sure. But then after a little time passes, we find ourselves laughing and forgetting what we were mad about. The other day, she made a comment that reminded me of something I had been irritated about, and I jokingly said, "I knew I was mad at you about something. Thanks for reminding me what it was!" We really try not to carry that weight of unforgiveness around each other. The reality is that not every offense is a minor one. And I'm not saying forgiveness is the easy way. It's the opposite. It's the path far less chosen. Forgiving someone who hurt you deeply doesn't mean you must allow them back into your life. Forgiveness is about the condition of *your* heart, not theirs—it's the path to a story lived in freedom and joy.

Forgiveness is hard, but carrying that burdensome load of unforgiveness is much harder. Remember that bitterness can make you sick, and heavy grudges are difficult to carry. I don't want my story to be one that keeps all these records of other people's wrongs. I want my story to be more than that. Jesus is calling you today to set down all of the unforgiveness you are carrying around in your heart. He wants to carry those burdens for you. I

believe Jesus wants to lighten your steps so you can journey toward parts of your story that really matter. Your
choice to forgive others the way God has forgiven you
will put His Glory on full display through your story.

CONNECT TO HIS STORY

Read the following passages and consider how they apply
to your life:

> **MATTHEW 6:14–15** *"For if you forgive other people when
> they sin against you, your heavenly Father will also forgive
> you. But if you do not forgive others their sins, your Father
> will not forgive your sins."*

> **MARK 11:25** *"And when you stand praying, if you hold any-
> thing against anyone, forgive them, so that your Father in
> heaven may forgive you your sins."*

Why do you think Jesus connects our forgiveness
with our heavenly Father forgiving us?

Paul encourages us that we should not sin in our
anger; he says we shouldn't hold on to anger and give the
devil a foothold. What does this say about forgiveness?

As you read these Scriptures about forgiveness, what
comes to mind? A person you know, perhaps? What
actions do you find difficult to forgive?

CRAFT YOUR STORY

Write about a situation where you have struggled with forgiveness this past year and how that has kept you from focusing on following Jesus. In what ways has that weighed you down? Write about the steps you need to take to move on and live in forgiveness.

SHARE YOUR STORY

Identify some moments where you have been forgiven in your own journey. How did that feel? How much more have you been forgiven by God? Take a moment to tell someone about the impact of God's forgiveness in your life.

LIVE YOUR STORY

Take a step toward focusing on what really matters—following Jesus—by extending forgiveness to someone. Whether it's for something big or something small, whether the person is still around or long gone, stop carrying that weight on your journey.

My Priorities, Your Glory

I read a book a while back that encouraged me to write my own eulogy. Of course, a eulogy is a summary of a person's life usually delivered or read at a funeral *after* they pass away. At first, I thought, *What a depressing exercise!* But I decided to give it a try anyway and quickly realized how meaningful and clarifying that little writing project could be. As I thought about how I wanted to be remembered, the first things I wrote down had nothing to do with my career. There was no mention of money, fame, the things I owned, hit songs, gold records, or critical praise. Instead, I wrote about a different set of priorities—things that are vital to my legacy, such as how I love my family and the ways my life has touched people and changed the world for the better. This exercise helped me focus on the meaningful moments that will last, and most of it revolved around my deep desire to follow Jesus.

I keep that self-written eulogy and read it most mornings. The idea is to start each day by beginning with the end in mind, asking myself, *What if today is my last day? How do I want to be remembered?* This powerful meditation has helped me focus on more eternal priorities. The whole exercise reminded me of Paul's words in 2 Timothy 4:7 where he seems to have penned a bit of a first-person eulogy himself: "I have fought the good fight, I have finished the race, I have kept the faith." I want people to say that about me, don't you? I want to fight the good fight, finish the race, and keep the faith. But I know there is only one way I can do this: I have to choose to follow Jesus each and every day.

I love the Bible story when the disciples are out fishing and they respond to Jesus's call. They are just doing their jobs, working to make ends meet, trying to pay the bills and take care of their responsibilities in the same ways we do. I sometimes wonder if Simon Peter rolled out of bed that day and laced up his sandals dreading a long, hot day on the water. Maybe James was stressed because he was behind on rent. Maybe John had a fight with his parents over breakfast that morning. Did they have to get to work early and patch up the boat to get it seaworthy for the day? The three of them had dropped out of school at this point, and fishing was probably going to be their life's work—that is, until Jesus arrived. When we read that story, we don't often consider that Jesus is breaking into their daily routine and asking them to give up the comfort of the lives they know. But that is exactly where the good fight, the race, the faith begins—by following Jesus.

The question of "What if today is my last day?" sharpens my focus to let go of my priorities and embrace God's. Am I doing the things that Jesus wants me to do? Do I have a clear vision for the race God is calling me to run? Today, maybe imagine yourself in that fishing boat . . . will your eulogy ultimately tell the story of how you dropped your nets and followed Jesus? Are you focused on the priorities that will lead to an eternal story? Are your priorities bringing glory to God today?

CONNECT TO HIS STORY

Read the following passages and consider how they apply to your life:

LUKE 5:1-11 *"One day as Jesus was standing by the Lake of Gennesaret, the people were crowding around him and listening to the word of God. He saw at the water's edge two boats, left there by the fishermen, who were washing their nets. He got into one of the boats, the one belonging to Simon, and asked him to put out a little from shore. Then he sat down and taught the people from the boat. When he* *had finished speaking, he said to Simon, 'Put out into deep water, and let down the nets for a catch.' Simon answered, 'Master, we've worked hard all night and haven't caught anything. But because you say so, I will let down the nets.' When they had done so, they caught such a large number of fish that their nets began to break. So they signaled their partners in the other boat to come and help them, and they came and filled both boats so full that they began to sink. When Simon Peter saw this, he fell at Jesus' knees and said, 'Go away from me, Lord; I am a sinful man!' For he and all his companions were astonished at the catch of fish they had taken, and so were James and John, the sons of Zebedee, Simon's partners. Then Jesus said to Simon, 'Don't be afraid; from now on you will fish for people.' So they pulled their boats up on shore, left everything and followed him."*

2 TIMOTHY 4:7-8 *"I have fought the good fight, I have finished the race, I have kept the faith. Now there is in store for me the crown of righteousness, which the Lord, the righteous Judge, will award to me on that day—and not only to me, but also to all who have longed for his appearing."*

How do these two readings—the response by the disciples and the "eulogy" moment by Paul—speak to God's calling in your life?

Luke tells us Simon Peter, James, and John simply "left everything" and followed Him. There was no hesitation, no anxiety, no complaining—they just responded. What can this teach us about the importance of obedience?

How is Jesus calling you to fish for people? What does it mean for you to "run the good race" today?

CRAFT YOUR STORY

Spend some time writing your own eulogy. Think about the things that matter in your life and for what you most want to be remembered. Would people remember you for following Jesus?

SHARE YOUR STORY

Write about a moment in your life when Jesus called to you. How did you respond? What was that moment like for you? Share your story with three people today.

LIVE YOUR STORY

As you reflect on your personal eulogy and think about God's calling in your life, you're reminded of some things you've overlooked. Write down three things that you want to make a *priority* today as you follow Jesus, and go out and make sure you do one before the sun goes down. Maybe you want to encourage someone or pray for someone. Maybe you need to spend more time with your family. Maybe God is calling you to something big, like a career change. Whatever it is, take a step in that direction today.

NOTES

My Broken Road, His Glory

Sometimes I am overwhelmed by God's grace when I look at my life. We probably have all been through times in our journey when we feel like saying, "*My* story, Lord? Can You really use a story this broken?" I wonder if at any point in your life, have you been defeated enough to ask God a question like that?

We have talked about how guilt and shame are powerful tools the enemy will use to separate you from God. Guilt lies about our identity as a son or daughter of the King. Shame tells us we don't belong in His house, at His table. It is a strategy of the enemy to convince us we belong on the outside looking in. But that is a lie—it simply is not what the Bible teaches.

When we read a book, watch a movie, or experience any story, we might naturally find ourselves identifying with one or more of the characters. The same happens when I read Scripture, especially with the story Jesus tells in Luke 15 about the prodigal son. I have to be honest . . . if I had only one passage in the Bible I could preach to my kids, to my friends, to myself, or to the world, it would always be the story of this lost son coming home. Why? Because I've been the prodigal so many times, trying to journey out on my own, to earn my own way, making mistakes, striking out, and then wondering if my Father would forgive me and take me back. And these days, as a dad, I get to stand in a father's shoes. I understand that love—one so deep that no matter how my children might hurt me, I would always welcome them back with open arms.

Of course, my favorite part of the story about the prodigal is found in the sentence about the son's return, "while he was still a long way off" (verse 20). Why? Because at that distance the father *ran* to meet his son. Romans 5:8 tells us how God demonstrates His love: while we were still sinners (a long way off . . .), Christ died for us.

Perhaps you've been hiding in the shadows of the steeple and feel like you don't belong inside the walls of the church or inside the arms of the loving Father because of the broken road you've walked. You need to hear that God sees you and runs to meet you no matter where you are and what you have done. He's already gone as far as He needed to go to save you, all the way to a cross.

Maybe you are at a point in your story where you are convinced you don't belong. You should know that Jesus did
His best work with the people who were the "religious
outsiders." He was on a mission to reach those who were
convinced they didn't belong, and He welcomed them as
part of the family of God.

You see, God's grace always leads to glory. The freedom found in God's mercy is a consistent message: "You
are welcome here. You belong in your Father's house—no
matter how far you have wandered away." Today, I hope
that you can allow that truth to be a turning point in your
story. Maybe it is time to turn from the direction you've
been running and come toward your Father's house. I
promise: you will see Him running to embrace you. No
matter how broken your road may seem, His grace is
always drawing you back to the story of redemption He
is writing with your life.

CONNECT TO HIS STORY

Read the following passage and consider how it applies
to your life:

> **LUKE 15:17–21** *"When he came to his senses, he said, 'How
> many of my father's hired servants have food to spare, and
> here I am starving to death! I will set out and go back to my
> father and say to him: Father, I have sinned against heaven
> and against you. I am no longer worthy to be called your*

son; make me like one of your hired servants.' So he got up and went to his father. But while he was still a long way off, his father saw him and was filled with compassion for him; he ran to his son, threw his arms around him and kissed him. The son said to him, 'Father, I have sinned against heaven and against you. I am no longer worthy to be called your son.'"

Have you ever identified with the son in this story?

What is the catalyst for the son to return home?

In ancient cultures it would be considered unseemly for the head of a household to run anywhere. What does it say about the father's love (and God's love for you) that he doesn't just accept the son back into his home—he lowers himself to run to greet him?

CRAFT YOUR STORY

Have you ever had a moment when you felt as if you were on the outside of the Father's house looking in? How does the story of the father running to meet his prodigal son speak to you in your own life today? Write about a prodigal moment in your own life and how the heavenly Father ran to embrace you and bring you home no matter how broken your road seemed at the time. Maybe you are reading this today and feel like you can't come home. Read the full story of the prodigal in Luke 15:11–32.

What can you learn about God's grace for you through this parable?

SHARE YOUR STORY

Think about the prodigal people in your own life. Maybe you know someone who has been the hands and feet of Jesus and helped welcome you back when you wandered off. Take a moment to thank that person today for being there for you. Maybe someone else in your life feels that he or she cannot return to God and needs to hear the story of God's unconditional love and grace in your life. Take a moment to write a note to this person sharing what God has done to welcome you back.

LIVE YOUR STORY

Today, list the ways God has extended grace into your life and brought you home on that broken road. Write down three ways you can extend that same grace to others in your life this week.

NOTES

DAY 16

My Freedom, Your Glory

Have you ever been to a shopping mall right as it's about to open or in the evening before closing? The stores in older malls used to have gates that they could pull down and lock over the entrance to a store. When I was a kid growing up in Chicago, I had an irrational fear of getting locked in one of those stores at closing time. I remember holding on to my mom when I was little as the shop owners started to lower those gates, terrified that I would be imprisoned in a Sears or a Hallmark store for the night.

I had a similar sensation as an adult when my redeye flight out of Los Angeles got stuck at LAX. I found myself imprisoned in an airport for the night with all the other poor folks sleeping on the floor and using their jackets as pillows next to gate B7. Of course, it didn't matter which customer service rep I spoke to on the phone or how important my reason was for wanting to get home—nothing changed. I was sentenced to a long night inside that airport in California two thousand miles away from my family.

In reality, many of us live our lives in prisons of our own making. Sin, addiction, anger, hatred, jealousy—all of these things can trap us in our own misery. The enemy loves to lock us inside those kinds of gates, helpless to fix things on our own. But Jesus teaches in the Gospel of John that He is the way, the truth, and the life (14:6) and that "the truth will set you free" (8:32). Once we invite Jesus into our story, we are called into a life of freedom.

I get so inspired by the people I meet who are on their recovery journey because of the way they appreciate, practice, and celebrate their freedom from bondage. I'm so encouraged when I am out on the road and talk with folks who share how God transformed their lives by liberating them from the chains of addiction. I have one awesome fan who brings a poster to my concerts that celebrates how many days she has been sober. Can you imagine the joy we'd feel if we all celebrated the freedom Christ offers with the same enthusiasm?

Throughout the story of the Bible, Jesus heals people physically, but He is also always performing heart surgery. He talks about setting us free to live life to the fullest. He promises to set us free from sin so that we can experience joy. And the most important part of the Jesus work in our lives is that He *sets us free so we can love others.*

We regularly celebrate freedom in our country each Fourth of July with big fireworks, cookouts, and concerts with our family, friends, and community. But just think of the truth that you can celebrate God's freedom every single day! Every day we need to embrace the reality that Jesus has come to write freedom into our story—to open the gates and release us from the bondage and the burden of sin. What does it look like to celebrate the spiritual liberty Christ has bought for you for God's glory? What does it look like to truly be free to love and serve others? How can you use that freedom from sin to live a story that brings Him glory?

CONNECT TO HIS STORY

Read the following passage and consider how it applies to your life:

JOHN 8:31–36 *"To the Jews who had believed him, Jesus said, 'If you hold to my teaching, you are really my disciples. Then you will know the truth, and the truth will set you free.' They answered him, 'We are Abraham's descendants and have never been slaves of anyone. How can you say that we shall be set free?' Jesus replied, 'Very truly I tell you, everyone who sins is a slave to sin. Now a slave has no*

permanent place in the family, but a son belongs to it for-
ever. So if the Son sets you free, you will be free indeed."'

What requirement does Jesus give for being a disciple?

The religious teachers in this passage are confused about the freedom Jesus is talking about. What does Jesus say about sin?

What does this passage tell you about freedom as a central part of the good news of Jesus?

CRAFT YOUR STORY

Jesus is preaching to the religious crowd in this passage of John, and He doubles down that sin is slavery but that if He sets you free, then you are truly free. Spend some time today writing about the ways that Jesus has set you free with His work on the cross. What are some ways you've settled for a prison of your own making?

SHARE YOUR STORY

Our story is truly a story of freedom. We talk about and celebrate freedom often in our country, but how do you celebrate your freedom in Christ? Choose several people whom you are close to in your life and share with each of them a story of how Jesus has brought freedom into your daily life through His love and grace.

LIVE YOUR STORY

Jesus is clear in His teaching that we are free from sin once He has forgiven us. But the more we grow in our faith, the more God shows us areas of sin and bondage that He wants to liberate us from. Spend some moments in prayer today asking God to show you new areas of life that He is calling you to surrender to Him, and then begin walking into new freedom.

NOTES

My Promises, His Glory

Today I would like to ask for your prayers, and here's why: I am a girl dad. Not only that but my daughters have reached their teenage years and boys have started to circle the West house like sharks around a life raft. Honestly, the thought of my daughters starting to date hasn't worried me as much as it's made me even more aware of the example I'm setting for them in terms of what a godly man looks and acts like. Obviously, perfection is not possible as a parent, but I want to lead by example. I want to be faithful to God by keeping my promises. The older I get, the more I realize that people pay attention to what you *do* far more than what you say. I want my daughters to see in me a man who keeps the promises he made to their mother and to them. I want them to see a man who stays faithful in the way I treat other people, the way I try to care for my community, and in how I try to live a story that brings God glory. I want them to know I am true to my word, because I am showing them who God is—not just through my words but also with my actions.

I read a great story recently about a promise that C. S. Lewis made when he was young to his good friend Paddy Moore. Lewis promised to take care of Moore's wife and daughter if Moore should be killed in battle during World War I. He fulfilled that promise by looking after his friend's wife until she died and her daughter was grown. Of course, we live in a world where promises regularly go unkept. Political candidates often abandon pledges once they get elected. Big corporations tend to overpromise and underdeliver with false advertisements for their products and services. And we've all seen countless marriage vows broken.

Just imagine the impact we could make as God's people by simply keeping our promises—by doing what we say we will do. As I work to be a man of my word in both my personal and professional lives, I am grateful for the role model that my father was for me in the way he lived his life and conducted his ministry. I even wrote a song about my dad called "Looking Up" that talks about the example he set. The song is written from the perspective of a son who looks up to his dad only to discover that his dad is always looking up to God for guidance. Dad didn't tell me to follow Jesus. He *showed* me how to follow Jesus. That's the best example any of us could ever set for the ones in our lives whom we get the honor of influencing.

When I think about the responsibilities in my own life and the reality that I am far from perfect, I pray that people will see I am following through with following Jesus. Because the story that gives God glory *isn't* perfect; it simply reflects the character of Jesus. Keeping our promises means we keep looking to Him in every situation. And when it comes to God's character, He is who He says He is, and does what He says He will. He is a promise keeper. That's the story I want to write at home, at church, at work, and wherever I go in this world. Is that the story you are telling? Will those who know you best say that you keep your promises?

CONNECT TO HIS STORY

Read the following passage and consider how it applies to your life:

> **MATTHEW 5:33-37** *"Again, you have heard that it was said to the people long ago, 'Do not break your oath, but fulfill to the Lord the vows you have made.' But I tell you, do not swear an oath at all: either by heaven, for it is God's throne; or by the earth, for it is his footstool; or by Jerusalem, for*

> *it is the city of the Great King. And do not swear by your head, for you cannot make even one hair white or black. All you need to say is simply 'Yes' or 'No'; anything beyond this comes from the evil one."*

In this teaching, how does Jesus raise the bar on being faithful?

What does it mean to you to simply say *yes* or *no*? In what area of life do you need this teaching the most?

How can we reflect the character of God in the way we handle our words and promises?

What do you think Jesus means by connecting "anything beyond this" type of promise keeping to "the evil one"?

CRAFT YOUR STORY

Who are the promise keepers in your life? Who are the people who have modeled God's faithfulness in your story? Choose one and write about that person today. How can you model those qualities in your own life?

SHARE YOUR STORY

Reach out to the person you chose to write about and thank them for teaching you about God's faithfulness. Maybe you can even share the words you wrote about them.

LIVE YOUR STORY

Consider the promises that you make in your life—maybe a promise to your spouse, your children, your work. What is an area of promise that you can follow through on today? Identify several and take action. Remind people that your "yes is a yes" because the promises that we keep *matter*.

NOTES

My Past, Your Glory

Pastor Adam's dad was also his elementary school principal when he was growing up in West Virginia in the early 1980s. Adam tells a great story about a particular teacher who kept a list on one side of the blackboard specifically for anyone who broke a rule or misbehaved. It was literally called the "bad list." Adam recalls that if you missed homework, talked when you shouldn't talk, or got out of your seat when you weren't supposed to, you were forced to make the "walk of shame" and write your name on the board in front of everyone. Then those names would stay on the list all week long. Adam was pretty sure the janitor wiped the slate clean over the weekends. But whenever he had to put his name up on the board, he would go to school each day terrified that his dad, the principal, would see it.

I don't know about you, but sometimes, in my head, I find myself running down the list of wrongs I've committed. It is as if I keep a mental "bad list" on the blackboard of my mind. I think we all carry that list of our past wrongs around with us. There is a moment in the Gospel of John when the Pharisees bring a woman to Jesus who has been caught in the act of adultery. According to Jewish law, she is to be stoned. John tells us that Jesus kneels down and writes something in the sand and then challenges the Pharisees that they can cast a stone at this woman only if they are without sin. One by one they drop their stones and walk away. Jesus "erases the blackboard" for her. Jesus isn't interested in her past; he tells her to go and sin no more.

Grace and forgiveness are Jesus's way of turning the world upside down and rewriting our story, yet we are the ones who want to hang on to the mistakes of our past. Satan always wants to remind us of our list. The world wants to throw stones, but Jesus is there to tell us we are free.

I once watched an interview with a star NFL quarterback as he talked about remembering his career losses more than his wins. He could describe in great detail the big games that his team lost, and he said those games still haunt him. I've never stepped foot on an NFL football field or hoisted a Super Bowl trophy over my head, but I sure can relate to being haunted by past defeats. One day that same friend, Adam, asked his dad (now retired from being a principal) about the "bad list" in that teacher's classroom all those years ago. He told his dad how terrified and ashamed he would get that his name was written on that blackboard. When he explained how happy he was that the janitor erased the board every weekend, his dad smiled and said, "I was the one that would go in and erase all the students' names from that blackboard every Friday, son."

Even all these years later, that admission brought tears to Adam's eyes. As he went on to explain, Jesus does for us what his dad did for him and all his classmates in elementary school: He wipes our slate clean. He forgives and forgets our past. In 1 Corinthians 13:5 the apostle Paul reminds us that love "keeps no record of wrongs." When I struggle with my past, I wonder what it would be like if the only lists I kept were the ways saying that I am loved and forgiven and set free by God. That is the kind of story I want to live. That is the kind of story God is writing for you as well.

CONNECT TO HIS STORY

Read the following passage and consider how it applies to your life:

> **JOHN 8:2–11** *"At dawn he appeared again in the temple courts, where all the people gathered around him, and he sat down to teach them. The teachers of the law and*

*the Pharisees brought in a woman caught in adultery.
They made her stand before the group and said to Jesus,
'Teacher, this woman was caught in the act of adultery. In
the Law Moses commanded us to stone such women. Now
what do you say?' They were using this question as a trap,
in order to have a basis for accusing him. But Jesus bent
down and started to write on the ground with his finger.
When they kept on questioning him, he straightened up and
said to them, 'Let any one of you who is without sin be the
first to throw a stone at her.' Again he stooped down and
wrote on the ground. At this, those who heard began to go
away one at a time, the older ones first, until only Jesus was
left, with the woman still standing there. Jesus straightened
up and asked her, 'Woman, where are they? Has no one
condemned you?' 'No one, sir,' she said. 'Then neither do I
condemn you,' Jesus declared. 'Go now and leave your life
of sin.'"*

How does Jesus view the woman in this passage?

What do you imagine that Jesus leans down and writes in the sand?

Can you imagine how the woman felt as Jesus came to her defense? How often do you take time to recognize that He does the same for you?

What does this story teach us about grace?

CRAFT YOUR STORY

Think about the "list" you keep of your wrongdoings, your slip-ups, your failures. Consider how God sees those situations in your life according to Scripture. God is not the great scorekeeper. He isn't making a list of your wrongdoings; in fact, your past is part of your unique story of coming home to Him. Write about what it means to have your past—the good, the bad, and the ugly— truly redeemed and forgiven by Him.

SHARE YOUR STORY

It is so important to share with others the work God has done in our life. Find someone in your family, community, church, or small group to connect with and describe one of the ways that God has redeemed your past for His Glory.

LIVE YOUR STORY

This week, consider Jesus's interactions with the adulterous women. How can you be like Jesus to other people in the same way when they mess up? How can you share the story of your past and the love of Jesus with the world through the way you speak and act today?

NOTES

My Memory, Your Glory

My puppy, Rocky, is a Bernedoodle with a big personality. From what I can tell, he's the happiest dog I've ever met except when I leave the house. If Rocky had his way, I would stay home cuddling with him all day, every day. When I do leave the house, whether for a weekend of concerts, a family vacation, or even a quick run to the grocery store, Rocky greets me upon my return as if I've been gone for a year. His excitement is uncontrollable. He jumps up and down. He runs a lap around the house. He falls at my feet and lets out a cry of joy and relief as if to say, *THANK YOU THANK YOU, OH THANK YOU FOR SHOWING UP! I THOUGHT YOU'D NEVER GET HERE.*

Now, I'm no expert about what type of memory dogs have, but it doesn't matter how many times I've shown up at our home, he's forgotten all of that and wondered if I would ever show up again. I tend to be forgetful like Rocky when it comes to remembering God's track record of showing up in my life. But when I stop and allow my mind and heart to travel back through the story of my life, I am reminded that God is in the business of showing up. It's what He does.

Let's just recount the truth of Scripture: God showed up in a fiery furnace. He showed up in a lions' den. He showed up at the shore of the Red Sea when the greatest army in the world was bearing down on a ragtag group of helpless slaves. Sometimes God shows up in the very moment a desperate soul is hanging by the last thread of a worn-out rope.

Sometimes, however, the timing of His arrival might not line up with what we had hoped. When Jesus heard that His friend Lazarus was sick, He didn't arrive on the scene until Lazarus had already been dead for four days. Things seemed hopeless. But Jesus said, "This sickness will not end in death" (John 11:4). Lazarus was called from the grave and brought back to life when God showed up.

Can you imagine how often Martha must have told the story of what happened after Lazarus came back to life? I bet the whole town heard from Martha repeatedly about that time Jesus arrived a few days late and Lazarus woke up. We can all identify with Lazarus. Jesus has spoken into the tombs, the hopeless places, the darkness of our own stories and cried, "Come forth!" *Bam!* A new life! Imagine having *that* go-to story to share around the table. Mary, Martha, Lazarus, and everyone at that graveside had the *best* stories to tell at any party—some serious small talk about a big, *big* God.

When we take time to reflect on those God moments of our life and share them with others, we call forth that moment to the present. Just like Rocky, the Bernedoodle, we humans tend to forget God's faithfulness. We have to remind ourselves and remind one another of how Jesus shows up for us.

When I look back at my story, my mind and heart are flooded with the memories of so many moments when God showed up in my life. He showed up on a blue couch and knocked on the door of my heart as I watched a Billy Graham crusade and made the decision to follow Him. He showed up in a hospital room when I had emergency surgery on my vocal cords. He showed up in a delivery room twice, blessing me and my wife with healthy children despite difficult pregnancies. In desperate hours, weak moments, impossible situations, and anytime life has thrown something at me, God showed up.

So the question is, How have you seen Him show up in your life? I encourage you to focus on those moments and remember the perfection of God's timing. Hold those memories of God's faithfulness in your life close and share them as often as you can with others so you may return to them in moments when doubt, frustration, and trying times come creeping in. The story of Lazarus teaches us that not even something as final as a sealed tomb can separate us from the power of God's miracles. Jesus is going to show up in even the most upside-down, messed-up story and speak His hope into your life: "I'm here to help. I'll never leave you or forsake you. I know the plans I have for you."

CONNECT TO HIS STORY

Read the following passage and consider how it applies to your life:

> **JOHN 11:38-44** *"Jesus, once more deeply moved, came to the tomb. It was a cave with a stone laid across the entrance. 'Take away the stone,' he said. 'But, Lord,"* said Martha, the sister of the dead man, 'by this time there is a bad odor, for he has been there four days.' Then Jesus said, 'Did I not tell you that if you believe, you will see the glory of God?' So, they took away the stone. Then Jesus looked up and said, 'Father, I thank you that you have heard me. I knew that you always hear me, but I said this for the benefit of the people standing here, that they may believe that you sent me.' When he had said this, Jesus called in a loud voice, 'Lazarus, come out!' The dead man came out, his hands and feet wrapped with strips of linen, and a cloth around his face. Jesus said to them, 'Take off the grave clothes and let him go.'"*

How do you think Martha felt about Jesus showing up four days after His friend Lazarus had died? Do you remember a time when you were desperate for Jesus to show up? How did you handle it?

What does it mean when Jesus explains that His words are for "the benefit of the people standing here"?

What are some of the "tombs" (the dark, hopeless, or frustrating circumstances) that Jesus has called you out of in your life?

Jesus commands the onlookers to "take off the grave clothes" and free Lazarus. Are you still carrying the "grave clothes" from the places, sins, or situations from which Jesus has rescued you?

CRAFT YOUR STORY

In your *My Story* Journal, share the first moment you remember God really showing up in your life. Make sure to take time to explain every detail, such as, Who was there? Where and what did it all look and feel like? How did you feel when you recognized God's presence?

SHARE YOUR STORY

Make a list of five ways God has shown up in your life this year and share it with someone personally or on the popwe website to encourage others. Remember, God can use your story to change lives.

LIVE YOUR STORY

Thank God for those moments He showed up and brought deliverance. Ask Him to show you if you are hanging on to any "grave clothes" from those places.

NOTES

DAY 20

My Prayers, Your Glory

Have you ever been in a tough situation that left you without the words to pray? My friend Ryan went through a season where he lost his father, his younger sister and her unborn child, and his mother-in-law in the span of a few years. During that long run of grief, words seemed useless to him. As he tried to pray, no phrase, Scripture, or song seemed adequate to express what was going on in his inner life.

Have you ever been there? In a season of grief, loss, and pain? Perhaps the pages of your story are so painful, they leave you without words. Maybe you've prayed for healing from an illness, but you're still not well; you are desperate for a child to return home, but he or she is still lost; you long for the restoration of a relationship, but it

137

remains broken; you've begged God for the mercy of a hard season to be over, but there is still no end in sight.

Our losses in life can leave us at a loss for words.

When I was young, I believed I needed to pray a certain way. Growing up as a preacher's kid, I was often called on to pray in public. I believed that my prayers needed to live up to a certain standard—to be eloquent, emotional, inspirational. As a result, my prayers too often just felt like a performance. I wasn't trying to impress God as much as I was trying to impress those around me. But then life brought those times when I felt all alone— you know, the moments when life drags you to your knees involuntarily. When you're feeling weak, beaten up by the world, circling the drain of your circumstances, there is no room for flowery word salads of prayer. There is only room for the stark, unfettered truth.

In Psalms, David reminds us through his own mountaintop experiences and times of anguish and frustration that God doesn't require eloquence, He just wants our honesty. God hears our laments and pays attention to our cries. He hears our praise and our songs. Our prayers don't even need to be understandable; they just need to be true. In Exodus, the Bible tells us that God heard His people's groans—not their *words* but their *groans*. In Romans, Paul says the Holy Spirit knows us so intimately that He intercedes for us as we pray—even in those groans.

My friend Ryan says the moments in his grief journey when he couldn't find words to pray were the very moments he felt the arms of God wrapped around him. I also know people who have experienced the opposite: moments of such deep joy they couldn't find words adequate enough to thank Him. But God doesn't need our eloquent words or religious phrases. He responds to our open hearts. As we look through the pages of the Bible, we see how God leans in closer whenever we are at a loss for words. How reassuring that, in both the darkest seasons and those most joyous, He is present with us. We can be still and know He is God. We can witness His Glory in the nearness of His presence.

CONNECT TO HIS STORY

Read the following passages and consider how they apply to your life:

EXODUS 2:23-24 *"During those many days the king of Egypt died, and the people of Israel groaned because of their slavery and cried out for help. Their cry for rescue from slavery came up to God. And God heard their groaning, and God remembered his covenant with Abraham, with Isaac, and with Jacob" (ESV).*

ROMANS 8:26 *"In the same way, the Spirit helps us in our weakness. We do not know what we ought to pray for,*

*but the Spirit himself intercedes for us through wordless
groans."*

Can you identify with a moment in your life when
you were at a loss for words in prayer?

What does it mean to you that God heard Israel's
groan while the Israelites were in slavery?

What comfort can it bring to understand that the
Spirit intercedes for you with "wordless groans" in times
of pain and weakness?

CRAFT YOUR STORY

Write about a time in your life or season that was so difficult that you were often at a loss for words. What did you
learn about yourself and God through that time? Write
about ways that you experienced the presence of God in
those moments.

SHARE YOUR STORY

Have you ever experienced a time of prayer when you felt
God in the silence? Think about a difficult time when
God came near and share it with your small group, a close
friend, or someone in your faith community. Describe
God's presence in those moments to someone—how did
it feel?

LIVE YOUR STORY

Today if you are in a hard season, spend some time in silence before God. Set aside ten minutes to listen for Him. We are called to be Jesus to one another. Jesus sits with us in times of difficulty just as we should do for others. Reach out to someone going through a difficult season and just be in their presence—don't try to offer words of wisdom or encouragement, just sit and listen.

NOTES

My Battles, Your Glory

Every one of us will face a chapter dominated by life's battles, even if we haven't already. I vividly remember the day I was told I would undergo career-threatening vocal cord surgery. In that fear-filled moment sitting in the doctor's office, I was incapable of seeing any blessing that could come from that news. I felt confused and frustrated that my music ministry could be over. I knew I was in for a fight. I was up against a physical battle that would force me to be literally silent and then slowly retrain my voice to sing, unsure of whether I would ever fully recover. I faced the mental battle of trying to stay positive and fend off the depression and discouragement that can creep in when life isn't going the way you want. I also faced the spiritual battle of learning how to surrender to God's plan. Yes, all I saw were the battles I would be fighting and a long, hard road ahead.

But looking back now on that chapter of my story—that *silent* season when I was unable to talk or sing—I find it difficult to even remember the battle because there were so many . . . blessings. The blessing of peace washed over me like I had never experienced before. I received the blessing of learning how to persevere and the blessing of seeing God provide for my family while I was unable to work. Ultimately, there came the blessing of God healing my voice so I could once again step on stage and tell my story for His Glory. And that's just a small sample of the long list of blessings that flowed from that one battle in my life.

How about you? Have you faced a battle? If so, have you taken the time to look back on it and consider the blessings that emerged? Most of the time we can't see blessings when we are *in* the middle of the fight. But looking back, we can see God's glory on display as He brings us through those hard seasons. We can see how He shapes our character. In 2 Corinthians 12:1–10, the apostle Paul writes about the difficult seasons of his life and the "thorn in [his] flesh"—something that seems a weakness he cannot conquer. After noting how God's power is made perfect in weakness, he writes, "When I am weak, then I am strong."

For us, too, God uses hardships and difficult times as a pathway to develop our inner strength and learn to recognize His blessings.

Yes, we might feel weakened by the battles of a hard season, but there's a deep inner strength being built through these times of struggle. Maybe difficult seasons are like doing exercises—"spiritual planks" that strengthen our character, our mind, our heart, and our trust in God. I want to challenge you today to look back on even the battles you feel you've lost and consider what you gained. If you're reading these words right now, that means you're still here and you're still standing! We serve a God who promises to work all things for the good of those who love Him and are called according to His purpose (Romans 8:28). So ask yourself: *Do I love Him? Do I believe I am called according to His purpose?* If your answer is yes to both, then you can face any battle with confidence that it will not end in defeat. Your battles will lead to blessings. And your blessings will write the stories that bring God glory every time you tell them.

CONNECT TO HIS STORY

Read the following passages and consider how they apply to your life:

2 CORINTHIANS 12:5-10 *"I will not boast about myself, except about my weaknesses. Even if I should choose to* *boast, I would not be a fool, because I would be speaking the truth. But I refrain, so no one will think more of me than is warranted by what I do or say, or because of these surpassingly great revelations. Therefore, in order to keep me from becoming conceited, I was given a thorn in my flesh, a messenger of Satan, to torment me. Three times I pleaded with the Lord to take it away from me. But he said to me, 'My grace is sufficient for you, for my power is made perfect in weakness.' Therefore I will boast all the more gladly about my weaknesses, so that Christ's power may rest on me. That is why, for Christ's sake, I delight in weaknesses, in insults, in hardships, in persecutions, in difficulties. For when I am weak, then I am strong."*

ROMANS 8:28 *"And we know that in all things God works for the good of those who love him, who have been called according to his purpose."*

What does Paul's insistence that God's power is made perfect in our weakness mean to you today? What does it mean that Paul explains when he is weak, then he is strong?

What is an area of struggle that you are facing today? Do you believe what Paul writes in Romans, that God is working for the good—even in this hard season that you are facing?

What can these two Scriptures teach you about yourself in times of difficulty?

CRAFT YOUR STORY

We often can't see our growth in the middle of difficult circumstances. Reflect on a hard season of your life that you can look back on with some perspective and write down three things you learned about yourself and God during that time. How did that season strengthen your faith? What did God teach you about His love during that time?

SHARE YOUR STORY

Who walked with you during that hard season of life? Reach out to someone in your family, faith community, or small group and share three ways God used that season to change your life. If you are still struggling to recognize any good from a difficult season, ask someone to pray with you that God will show you how His hand is on your life during that time.

LIVE YOUR STORY

We often think that our journey is unique or unusual— that no one else can possibly relate to us. The reality is that we are surrounded by people who are facing the same hard seasons we have already been through. Today, take that list of three things you learned about God and yourself during your hard time and pray that God will bring people into your life who need to hear those lessons. Who in your family, small group, faith community, or neighborhood is going through a similar season? How can you lift them up today?

NOTES

My Rest, Your Glory

Who really likes the word *less*? Certainly not me. The definition of *less* is "a smaller amount of; not as much." Nobody likes less ice cream, less vacation time, less money, or less sunshine. When I see *less* attached to anything, it usually translates as "less fun." Especially when those four little depressing letters are attached to the word *rest*—as in *restless*. (If anything is added to *rest*, I'd much prefer "ful"—*restful*).

While I struggle with finding rest in my life, taking naps is a small rest strategy that I have conquered. A random rainy Wednesday afternoon? Sounds like a good time to nap! After church I hit the couch and turn on a football game . . . you guessed it—it's naptime. On the beach with the family? I'm napping! In all seriousness, though, most of us these days would define our daily life as rest*less*. And while I am an expert napper, most of the time I find truly resting to be a real challenge.

We know instinctively that rest is essential to a healthy life. Think about how irritable you can be when you feel restless. Not much feels worse than running yourself down and not being able to recharge. What about that weariness that can't be remedied with a nap or a good night's sleep? Few motivational Instagram posts hype the importance of resting up. We seem to live in a restless culture. Just think about how we spend our time celebrating busyness and complimenting the people who "grind" nonstop. I don't know about you, but even when I try to set aside time to rest, I can still get consumed with my never-ending to-do lists. Hard work is good, but hard work without real rest leads to physical, emotional, and even spiritual exhaustion.

So what does the Bible say about rest? Well, God sets the example for us in Genesis when He creates the world in six days of work and then, on the seventh day, rests. In the book of Exodus, right after God delivers Israel from their life of working *seven days a week* for the Egyptians, He mandates a full day for His people to rest (16:30).

But where do we go to rest when we live in a world with constant busyness, glorified productivity, and 24-7 access to everything? How do we find space to embrace a rest*ful* spirit? The answer is simple: we need to go to Jesus, the author of our story, for true rest. As St. Augustine once wrote in *The Confessions*, "For Thou hast made us for Thyself and our hearts are restless until they rest in Thee."*

In a world of chronic restlessness where busyness is the status quo, we often forget that we follow the God who offers rest. Jesus said, "Come unto me . . . and I will give you rest" (Matthew 11:28, KJV). This is such a beautiful offering. Jesus doesn't promise that He will finish that overdue project for you, shorten your to-do list, or deliver timely answers to the nagging questions keeping you awake last night. But He does promise rest—rest that is truer and more fulfilling than an afternoon nap.

Resting in God means moving through the world in a way that is the opposite of restlessness. Rest means knowing that Jesus is in control and walking with you every minute of the day. Rest feels like breathing in His presence and surrendering your worries. It involves pausing amid the hustle of your day and allowing Him to fill you with His presence. Rest is the posture of knowing there is a bigger story unfolding beyond what you can see. Rest begins by acknowledging you are defined not by what you do but by your identity as part of a royal priesthood (1 Peter 2:9). You can *rest* with the knowledge that God loves you unconditionally and that love is unrelated to your to-do lists or anything you need to accomplish today.

----

* *The Confessions*, trans. Frank Sheed (New York: Sheed & Ward, 1943).

Rest in the truth that you are not a human *doing*—God made you to be a human *being*. He is working through your story. Accept His invitation to rest in His presence today. Even your rest can bring Him glory.

CONNECT TO HIS STORY

Read the following passage and consider how it applies to your life:

> **PSALM 62:5–8** *"Yes, my soul, find rest in God; my hope comes from him. Truly he is my rock and my salvation; he is my fortress, I will not be shaken. My salvation and my honor depend on God; he is my mighty rock, my refuge. Trust in him at all times, you people; pour out your hearts to him, for God is our refuge."*

As you read this passage, consider all the reasons the psalmist finds rest in God.

What does the word *refuge* mean to you? How often do you see God as a refuge?

According to this passage, why is trust essential to rest?

CRAFT YOUR STORY

Write about a time when you experienced true rest in the presence of God and the knowledge that He loves you unconditionally. How did that happen? How did it empower you to be the person He has called you to be? What can you do to find that place of rest in Him today?

SHARE YOUR STORY

Find someone in your life who is experiencing a time of restlessness. Share the ways God has provided rest in your life.

LIVE YOUR STORY

Spend some time examining the areas of your life that make you feel restless, and pray about surrendering those things to God. How can you learn to rest in Him?

NOTES

My Imperfections, Your Glory

We live in a world that seems to thrive on making us feel as if we aren't enough. I read recently that the average person in America is exposed to thousands of advertisements every day. And guess what? They're *designed* to make us feel like we aren't enough (unless we buy what they are selling, of course). Social media doesn't help either—with all its filters and inaccurate representations of people's lives.

Honestly, we all naturally struggle with ideas about our "imperfections" without any outside help. We often feel like there is something wrong with who we are or how we are made. Not tall enough, attractive enough, smart enough, popular enough, athletic enough, or skinny enough. Just. Not. Enough. So we fixate on these areas as problems that need solving, leaving each of us to feel a degree of insecurity, no matter how confident we appear.

In the beginning of my music career, I was so insecure that I wouldn't allow the record label to put my face on the cover of my own album! Insecurity is something I've dealt with most of my life. I could cite a dozen things I wish were different about me, and I bet you could quickly list things you'd like to change about yourself too. But I want to challenge you today to consider that maybe the only thing imperfect is the way you see yourself. As I read through my Bible, I am reminded that what we regard as imperfect may in fact be perfect in God's eyes. I focus on the truth of Psalm 139:14: "I praise you because I am fearfully and wonderfully made; your works are wonderful, I know that full well."

What if these things we believe are imperfections are part of God's unique design for our story and for His Glory?

No matter what you believe about yourself—no matter how imperfect you believe you are—God made you wonderfully and with deep purpose. Whenever I think about my shortcomings or imperfections, I'm reminded of the story of Moses in Exodus. God chose Moses to lead His people out of slavery, but when He tells Moses to talk to Pharaoh, Moses throws a fit. He tries to get out of it by explaining to God that he can't speak well enough to pull it off. The thing is, God already has a plan involving the little things that Moses sees as imperfections. God tells Moses to take his brother, Aaron, along and let *him* do the talking so that together they can fulfill God's mission. What Moses views as a personal weakness, God uses to tell a better story. Maybe this was part of God's plan for Aaron to become Moses's right-hand man as they worked to liberate Israel and lead them out of Egypt.

When I look back on my own story, all the imperfections I was convinced needed to change have somehow been the very things that have put me right where I am today. Maybe what we think are the "less-than-perfect" parts of ourselves are the exact parts that allow us to trust God with our story. We then pray that God will work through every limitation or imperfection; we trust Him and wait to be a witness to what the Author of our story will do.

So before you get too caught up thinking about all the things you see as shortcomings, disabilities, or limitations, lean on God and trust the reality that you not only are *fearfully and wonderfully made* but also have been perfectly designed to play your part in the story He is writing to redeem the world.

CONNECT TO HIS STORY

Read the following passage and consider how it applies to your life:

> **EXODUS 4:10-17** *"Moses said to the LORD, 'Pardon your servant, Lord. I have never been eloquent, neither in the past nor since you have spoken to your servant. I am slow of speech and tongue.' The LORD said to him, 'Who gave human beings their mouths? Who makes them deaf or mute? Who gives them sight or makes them blind? Is it not I, the LORD? Now go; I will help you speak and will teach you what to say.' But Moses said, 'Pardon your servant, Lord. Please send someone else.' Then the LORD's anger burned against Moses and he said, 'What about your brother, Aaron the Levite? I know he can speak well. He is already on his way to meet you, and he will be glad to see you. You shall speak to him and put words in his mouth; I will help both of you speak and will teach you what to do. He will speak to the people for you, and it will be as if he were your mouth and as if you were God to him. But take this staff in your hand so you can perform the signs with it.'"*

How does God respond to Moses's objection? What does that say about how God sees what we believe are imperfections?

Consider the things in your own life that you consider "imperfections" like Moses's speech. How do you think God views those (according to His response to Moses in this passage)?

What does this passage teach about God's plans for His people? What does it teach about the kind of people God can use to do His work in the world?

CRAFT YOUR STORY

Spend time thinking about an "imperfection" in your life that you find yourself obsessing over. Remember that you are fearfully and wonderfully made. Spend some time writing about how God sees you and how He may use the things you find to be shortcomings or imperfections to spread the good news of His love to your family, friends, and community.

SHARE YOUR STORY

So often we just can't see ourselves in the same way God (and the people in our lives who love us) see us. Talk with someone whom you trust about some things you find to be imperfections. Ask them how they see these same things in your life.

LIVE YOUR STORY

We are called to love as God loves us. How can you help other people understand that they are fearfully and wonderfully made? Take a few moments to share with a few people in your community how much you appreciate them—just the way God made them.

NOTES

My Belonging, Your Glory

I think everyone knows what it feels like to be ignored or forgotten. Few feelings in life wound the heart more than being unseen. Everyone can tell stories from middle school and high school about being left out, overlooked, or treated as if they didn't belong. I've read articles written by psychologists who say that children who feel ignored will act out just to get punished because even bad attention is better than no attention at all. When I was playing baseball while growing up, people repeated the age-old sports wisdom that I shouldn't worry if the coaches were yelling at me but should worry if they *weren't*. If the coaches were getting after me, it meant they were paying attention, I was important, and they wanted me to get better. Of course, I don't ever remember this advice convincing me that getting yelled at was fun.

A friend of mine tells the story about shopping in a busy department store during the Christmas holiday with his four-year-old son. As they walked toward the toy aisle, he stopped to look at something for his wife. He literally looked away from his son, Eli, for less than five seconds, and when he turned back, the little guy had vanished. Can you imagine a worse feeling as a parent? He frantically began to call Eli's name and run up and down the aisles. The store attendants quickly joined in. The store manager hit the emergency locks on the main outside doors to the large department store and made an announcement over the loudspeaker that the store was on lockdown because of a missing child. No one was going to leave until Eli was found. It was the most terrifying ten minutes of my friend's life as a dad, until a store attendant walked by a clothes rack and heard quiet giggling. My friend was too relieved to be mad or embarrassed by his son's behavior. He scooped him up in his arms in a big hug, and everyone cheered as he carried Eli out of the store.

I think God values us in exactly the same way. He would close the shop and stop everything to search for you if you were lost. In a famous poem by Francis Thomson called "The Hound of Heaven" published in 1893, the poet describes God as the "hound of heaven" because of the way He pursues us.* We are valuable to Him! In

---

* Francis Thompson, "*The Hound of Heaven*," 1859-1907. Published in 1890, periodical *Merry England*.

Matthew 18:12–14, Jesus tells a story that reflects our worth to God. He explains that we are so important He would leave His entire flock behind to search for us if we were lost.

The message of the Bible is that we belong to God. Yes, it can be easy sometimes to feel lost and forgotten. And we live in a world that often seems to go out of its way to make us feel small and insignificant. But the real story is that the creator of the universe, the painter of the sky, the orchestrator of life, the one who handpicked every star in the galaxy is looking at you today, this very moment as you read these words, and saying, "I see you, I *know* you, I *love* you, you *matter* to Me, and you *belong* to Me."

We have so many things attacking our self-worth in today's world. Remember, God keeps coming to find us and remind us that we belong to Him. The fact that God is thinking of you all the time can be almost too much to comprehend, but it's the knowledge that He is mindful of us that truly changes everything. Just this realization alone can fill our stories with so much purpose. Our stories matter because we matter to God. You are on His mind today. You are not ignored or lost. You are not forgotten. Your story has significance because you are significant to Him. Your story has power because a powerful God says so. Today let's allow that knowledge to put power in our steps as we walk through this day.

CONNECT TO HIS STORY

Read the following passage and consider how it applies to your life:

> **MATTHEW 18:10-14** *"See that you do not despise one of these little ones. For I tell you that their angels in heaven always see the face of my Father in heaven. What do you think? If a man owns a hundred sheep, and one of them wanders away, will he not leave the ninety-nine on the hills and go to look for the one that wandered off? And if he finds it, truly I tell you, he is happier about that one sheep than about the ninety-nine that did not wander off. In the same way your Father in heaven is not willing that any of these little ones should perish."*

How does God feel about the lost?

Have you experienced a time in your life when you have felt like the lost sheep? How have you participated in looking for someone who was lost?

What does it look like to celebrate those who are found in our family, community, and neighborhood? How often do we do that?

Consider how this passage should shape your actions toward others.

CRAFT YOUR STORY

Write about a time—maybe a specific moment—when you realized that God came looking for you and reminded you that you belong to Him. How did God speak that truth into your life? In what ways did it change how you live your life and serve other people?

SHARE YOUR STORY

Find someone in your family, your small group, your church, school, or community and share your testimony of that moment when God came looking for you.

LIVE YOUR STORY

Take some time to reach out to someone who is lost or might feel left out in some way. Share the love of God and remind them that they belong to Him.

NOTES

My Contentment, Your Glory

Every story is touched by the good and the bad, the brokenness and the joy. We often recognize how God is present with us in those extreme situations—the highest highs and lowest lows of our story. But what about the middle-of-the-road moments? The pages and pages of life where it seems as if nothing noteworthy or significant happens? Are we content in those times when we seem to be in between the mountains and valleys? I often find those are the parts of my story when I am most tempted to go looking for joy outside of the good news of the gospel. The reality is that those days spent "in between" gather to make up the majority of our life's story. But do we acknowledge the gift of God's faithfulness and presence in those routine seasons of our life? Do we embrace contentment in those long, uneventful chapters?

I watched a documentary called *Happy*, created by Roko Belic and famous movie director Tom Shadyac, that made me think about my contentment. Tom achieved incredible wealth and status directing blockbuster hit movies such as *Ace Ventura: Pet Detective*, *The Nutty Professor*, and *Bruce Almighty*. He was living in a multimillion-dollar mansion surrounded by all the earthly possessions a person could ever dream about. Yet he was completely and utterly unhappy. He finally sold the mansion, sold all his possessions, and went on a quest to discover what it takes to find true happiness.

We know money isn't the answer, and buying more things doesn't give you a fulfilling life. If you doubt me, you can just go back and watch the old "Stuff Mart" episode of *Veggie Tales* when Bob the Tomato realized that buying more stuff wouldn't bring him happiness. Contentment doesn't come from busyness either—even though it is a modern-day "badge of success." I wonder if being busy isn't just another distraction that keeps us from recognizing God's gifts in the "normal times" of our life. The apostle Paul talks about the importance of being content, but I think most of us live in a constant state of *dis*content. We are always chasing that next thing we believe will make us happy, like a greyhound chasing that fake rabbit around a racetrack.

In Philippians 4:12, Paul writes that he has "learned the secret of being content in any and every situation."

Such contentment is found when we look for and pay attention to God in the everydayness of our lives. God isn't just present in the emotions of huge church gatherings or the singing and dancing at concerts. He isn't just there in the deep sadness of funerals or the desperation of hospital visits. He isn't just there in times of deep consequence like our mission trips.

Finding the kind of contentment Paul writes about means that we acknowledge God's presence in our daily routines. He says He will *always* be with us—that means in the times when I drop my daughter off at school, the random conversations with a stranger at the store, a morning cup of coffee when the house is quiet, and those evening walks with my wife. What if contentment starts with recognizing the presence of God in those "everything in-between" moments? What if God's gift of a beautifully meaningful story is unfolding right in front of us, and we just need to notice? The story that gives God glory doesn't include only highs and lows. He is right there with us in the routines and in-betweens of our life.

CONNECT TO HIS STORY

Read the following passage and consider how it applies to your life:

PHILIPPIANS 4:10-13 *"I rejoiced greatly in the Lord that at last you renewed your concern for me. Indeed, you were concerned, but you had no opportunity to show it. I am not saying this because I am in need, for I have learned to be content whatever the circumstances. I know what it is to be in need, and I know what it is to have plenty. I have learned the secret of being content in any and every situation, whether well fed or hungry, whether living in plenty or in want. I can do all this through him who gives me strength."*

What does it mean to you that Paul says he can be content in whatever circumstances?

Can you identify with some of the experiences Paul talks about in this passage? How and when?

Are you able to feel content in whatever circumstances you are in? Do you recognize God's presence in every circumstance?

CRAFT YOUR STORY

Write about a time in the past year where you felt happy and content. Looking back on that time, consider some ways that God was present with you through the "everydayness" of it.

SHARE YOUR STORY

Make a list of all the reasons you have to be content right now and share that list with someone close to you today.

So often, God's blessings are right there if we will just take the time to reflect and see.

LIVE YOUR STORY

Set three alarms on your watch or phone today for mid-morning, afternoon, and evening. When the alarm goes off, take a moment to pay attention to the blessings right then and all God's goodness in-between. Breathe in the day and thank God for His faithfulness.

NOTES

My Revisions, Your Glory

Before I became an author, I imagined that I'd spend most of my time *writing* as I worked on a book. But I've learned that making *revisions* is perhaps the biggest part of the writing process. That's because once you turn in that final manuscript, you don't get to take it back or make changes. Sometimes the difficult part is accepting the changes that my editors tell me need to be made. It takes a little humility. Once my book hits the shelves of the bookstore, it is what it is; that paragraph in chapter 3 is there forever. While the music process is a little bit different, most of the time your final take on a song is just as final as a book on the shelf. That is, until I was unexpectedly given the task of revising lyrics to an older song that a friend and I had written.

The song had already been out for a while, so, naturally, I believed we were finished working on it. But the
record company wanted us to create a new version for
radio airplay (some call it a radio edit). At first, the idea
of revising a good song felt too difficult of a challenge
for me to wrap my head around. The song had sounded
one way for so long that it was hard to imagine a different direction or approach. But once my friend and I
took those first steps into the revision process, guess what
happened? We landed on some new lyrics that we loved.
We were able to send the song in an awesome (and unexpected) new direction despite our fears or hesitation that
it couldn't be done.

I think we face the same challenge with the stories of
our lives. Maybe you know there's something that needs
to change in your life, but you've done things a certain
way for so long, it's hard to imagine changing. Or maybe
you've relied on the same crutch, held on to a bad habit,
settled for a dysfunctional relationship, or been physically
out of shape for so long that you can't envision change.
What if there is a version of you that you've lived with so
long it becomes comfortable, even though it isn't exactly
the life God wants for you? Of course, the easiest path
forward is always to ignore what needs to be revised and
settle for a story that never makes much-needed changes.
But that is the path of least resistance—and that just isn't
the way of Jesus.

I think that Jesus challenges us to revisit the story our life and rework the parts that need to be revised, not just for us but for those around us. While it is true that Jesus loves you just the way you are, it is also true that He loves you too much to let you stay just the way you are. I am still learning that following Jesus will require growth and change and transformation! There is a great story in the Gospels about a young man who comes to ask Jesus what he should do to get into the kingdom (Mark 10:17–22). Jesus looks at the young man and loves him, but He still provides life-changing advice: "Follow me." Because Jesus loves the rich young ruler way too much to let him stay that way.

If we are going to participate in the kingdom, we have to embrace the revisions Jesus wants to make in our life. As we take those first steps toward Him, we must trust that He is reworking our story day by day. He knows we are not the finished product or the best version of ourselves yet. But He is faithful and is calling you to take the first steps in His direction. The apostle Paul wrote of his confidence that "he who began a good work in you will carry it on to completion until the day of Christ Jesus" (Philippians 1:6).

As long as you are living and breathing, your story is not complete. Don't be afraid to revisit and rework the parts you know God wants to change. The closer you get to Jesus, the more you will find that He is working on each line of your life—bringing it closer and closer to the story that points the world to His grace, His love, and His Glory.

CONNECT TO HIS STORY

Read the following passage and consider how it applies to your life:

MARK 10:17-27 *"As Jesus started on his way, a man ran up to him and fell on his knees before him. 'Good teacher,' he asked, 'what must I do to inherit eternal life?' 'Why do you call me good?' Jesus answered. 'No one is good—except God alone. You know the commandments: "You shall not murder, you shall not commit adultery, you shall not steal, you shall not give false testimony, you shall not defraud, honor your father and mother."' 'Teacher,' he declared, 'all these I have kept since I was a boy.' Jesus looked at him and loved him. 'One thing you lack,' he said. 'Go, sell everything you have and give to the poor, and you will have treasure in heaven. Then come, follow me.' At this the man's face fell. He went away sad, because he had great wealth. Jesus looked around and said to his disciples, 'How hard it is for the rich to enter the kingdom of God!' The disciples were amazed at his words. But Jesus said again, 'Children, how hard it is to enter the kingdom of God! It is easier for a camel to go through the eye of a needle than for someone who is rich*

> *to enter the kingdom of God.' The disciples were even more amazed, and said to each other, 'Who then can be saved?' Jesus looked at them and said, 'With man this is impossible, but not with God; all things are possible with God.'"*

The passage explains, "Jesus looked at him and loved him" before Jesus challenges the man to change something in his life. What does that say about Jesus's love for us?

The young man lists all that he is doing right in his life, but Jesus requires more. How does this passage challenge you to follow Jesus?

What are some areas of revision in your life that are possible only with God?

CRAFT YOUR STORY

Write about an area of your life that you surrendered to God for revisions. How did making this change in your life bring you closer to following Jesus?

SHARE YOUR STORY

Part of following Jesus is being open to allowing Him to change our lives. Spend time today sharing with a friend, family member, or someone in your small group the ways that Jesus has revised your story for the better.

LIVE YOUR STORY

Spend some time in prayer asking God to show you what part of your story He wants to revise next. Write down some areas that you feel He might be calling you to change.

NOTES

My Legacy, His Glory

What do you hope to accomplish today? Do you have any big plans on the horizon? What are your work goals for the week?

Our culture spends a lot of time glorifying certain types of success and achievements and focusing on life's destinations. We look up to people with the most accomplishments, Instagram followers, money, and power. In my line of work, we celebrate platinum records—songs that are hitting the top of the charts every week—and books that make it to the bestseller list. These are the "greatest hits" of our life in the eyes of the world. But in reality, the most significant things we do in life can often seem like the least important things in the moment.

We learn a lot about what to value when we pay attention to Jesus. I often think about how Jesus did so many of His miracles while *on the way* to a destination somewhere else. And when we get too focused on worldly accomplishments, Jesus also points out in a story about the widow's offering (Mark 12:41–44) that His economy of greatness is far different. While the world's focus is on what we receive and achieve, God's focus is on the depth of our giving to others.

Reflecting on the values of Jesus makes me step back and ask myself some hard questions. How many times have I focused on earning more money so that my kids can have a better life, but I end up sacrificing moments with them to do that? Have I missed important ways to connect and help people because I was consumed with arriving at my destination? Do I sometimes focus on the big and the extravagant gestures of life instead of being faithful with my heart?

In the music industry, if an artist has had a successful career, it's common to compile a greatest hits collection. While this collection of songs might be the most highly regarded songs by the masses, most artists would probably say that their favorite songs were never the most popular. I know that's the case for me. Many of my favorite songs never made it to No. 1, but they still carry deep meaning that doesn't translate into chart-topping results. After all, the world's definition of success just doesn't hold up to God's definition of greatness.

I think about that truth whenever I read the story of the widow. I wonder how many big, flashy, greatest hits type of gifts were offered at the temple the day she gave her last two small copper coins. I think about Jesus healing the lepers "on the way" when I get too focused on getting to "destinations" in my daily life and career. You see, I believe that God's idea of our greatest hits is way more meaningful and lasting than our conceptions of what is great. He values the little things we do for others even when we are "on the way."

What if my "greatest hit" today wasn't the hours in the studio but taking time to cook breakfast for my wife? What if it wasn't the next big contract negotiation but canceling a meeting to take my daughter for ice cream? What if *your* greatest-hits moment is as simple as turning off your phone before walking in the house and choosing to be fully present with your family? Or what if the greatest thing you can do is buy a cup of coffee for a homeless person instead of rushing past him to your meeting? Maybe it is giving a little more than you can afford to someone in need today. Sometimes the smallest gift of your time or resources can have the biggest impact on eternity.

Let's build our legacy out of those eternal and lasting moments when we choose to give our hearts to God and our time and resources to others. When we focus on the things that matter to Jesus, we aren't just building our legacy, we are building His kingdom—and that is the story that brings God glory.

CONNECT TO HIS STORY

Read the following passages and consider how they apply to your life:

> **LUKE 17:11–14** *"Now on his way to Jerusalem, Jesus traveled along the border between Samaria and Galilee. As he was going into a village, ten men who had leprosy met him. They stood at a distance and called out in a loud voice, 'Jesus, Master, have pity on us!' When he saw them, he said, 'Go, show yourselves to the priests.' And as they went, they were cleansed."*

> **MARK 12:41–44** *"Jesus sat down opposite the place where the offerings were put and watched the crowd putting their money into the temple treasury. Many rich people threw in large amounts. But a poor widow came and put in two very small copper coins, worth only a few cents. Calling his disciples to him, Jesus said, 'Truly I tell you, this poor widow has put more into the treasury than all the others. They all gave out of their wealth; but she, out of her poverty, put in everything—all she had to live on.'"*

How do these two passages point to a difference between the way the world values time, wealth, and resources and the way we do?

How can the story of the lepers affect the way we look at what truly matters in our day? When you are on the way to your goals and destinations, are you looking for opportunities to help others?

In the story of the widow, what is Jesus teaching about the importance of giving? How can this change the way you think of giving in your own life?

CRAFT YOUR STORY

Spend some time writing down your greatest hits from the past year. What were your best accomplishments? How did they make you feel? Then write a list of your "eternal" greatest hits—the times when you went out of the way to serve others, to love others, or to give to others in a sacrificial way. Write about how that has changed you, your family, or your faith community.

SHARE YOUR STORY

Take time today to find someone whose greatest hit was taking time to offer you help in some way. Write a note, send a text, or call to thank that person.

LIVE YOUR STORY

Take some time today to pray that God will help you focus on greatest hits. Think of people in your life who need your help and commit not only to praying for them but also taking time to reach out with your energy, time, and resources. Pray that God will use you to make an eternal impact on others in your life.

NOTES

My Suffering, Your Glory

D o you remember that old Western movie called *The Good, the Bad and The Ugly*? I've always thought the title of that film pretty much sums up the different chapters that make up the stories of our lives. The book of Ecclesiastes points out that there is a season for everything. It is part of the human experience to live through seasons of joy *and* seasons of grief. No one makes it through life untouched by suffering. Maybe you have been there recently: a job loss, a spouse leaving, the passing of a loved one, a difficult diagnosis. Life often brings us face-to-face with suffering without explanation and sometimes leaves us wondering if God is still at work in our story. Throughout the Bible, we see that suffering is a by-product of the fallen world, a difficult but real part of life here on earth.

The apostle Paul was no stranger to suffering. Among other things he endured prison, beatings, and even a shipwreck. And yet in Romans 5:2–4 he explains how God can use our suffering to shape our stories and ultimately bring Him glory: "And we boast in the hope of the glory of God. Not only so, but we also glory in our sufferings, because we know that suffering produces perseverance; perseverance, character; and character, hope."

According to Paul, suffering refines our character, which enables us to lean on hope. And not just any hope—the hope of eternity. There is certainly so much suffering in the world that if we didn't look at it without the hope of eternity, I am not sure we could manage it. In Romans 8:18, Paul continues, "I consider that our present sufferings are not worth comparing with the glory that will be revealed in us."

I will never forget my friend Ron, who had ALS—a disease with no cure. He was in hospice care when we talked, and I was so moved that in the midst of his suffering he was focused on others. I had a Zoom call with Ron and planned on playing his favorite song of mine for him, but he had other plans for our time together. He spent most of his time in our conversation encouraging *me*. With his nurses by his side, he fought for his words but made every word count: "Matthew, God is using you!" "God is so proud of you." "Keep it up!"

Ron didn't know that I was struggling in a chapter of extreme discouragement at the time. Ron saw past his own fight with ALS and focused on lifting *me* up. When I received news of his passing, I was moved to write a song called "Wonderful Life," inspired by the way he embraced the beauty of this broken world and allowed God to produce perseverance, character, and hope through his suffering. In the midst of Ron's suffering, I saw a hope that was so vibrant and infectious that it touched everyone around him.

Ron showed me that this kind of hope can have an impact on how we carry our suffering. C. S. Lewis wrote in *The Problem of Pain*, "God whispers to us in our pleasures, speaks in our consciences, but shouts in our pains. It is his megaphone to rouse a deaf world."* God uses our suffering to wake us up to the suffering of others.

My friend Dawn suffered through drug and alcohol addiction for many years. Since going through recovery and committing her life to Jesus, she now helps others who are trapped in their addiction and desperate to find a way out. To the addicts who feels like no one understands, she says, "I know you, because I was you." I also think of Renee, who experienced the excruciating pain of losing her daughter in a drunk driving accident. Not

* C.S. Lewis, *The Problem of Pain*, (United Kingdom: The Centenary Press, 1940).

a day goes by that she doesn't long to see her daughter one more time. But as a result of her suffering, she has a desire to encourage others who have been victims.

We rightfully spend time talking about the goodness of God, but sometimes we don't recognize that the call to follow Jesus also means that we are to pick up the cross when we follow Him. Following Him does not ensure a lifetime of prosperity, health, and success; there will be chapters of suffering. Jesus loves us so much that He redeems us *through* our suffering. The One who carried our sins to a cross will show us how to use the devastating things we face in our life to lift up others. God's glory is on full display when the hope we find in our own suffering leads us to compassion for others who are suffering. That is how we bring heaven to earth. I am learning that God wants to use *every* piece of our story—the good, the bad, and, yes, even the ugly.

CONNECT TO HIS STORY

Read the following passage and consider how it applies to your life:

> **MARK 8:34-38** *"Then he called the crowd to him along with his disciples and said: 'Whoever wants to be my disciple must deny themselves and take up their cross and follow me. For whoever wants to save their life will lose it, but whoever loses their life for me and for the gospel will*

save it. What good is it for someone to gain the whole world, yet forfeit their soul? Or what can anyone give in exchange for their soul? If anyone is ashamed of me and my words in this adulterous and sinful generation, the Son of Man will be ashamed of them when he comes in his Father's glory with the holy angels.'"

How does this help us understand the suffering we go through in life?

When you have experienced seasons of suffering, how has Jesus, who suffered for you on the cross, come close to sustain you?

How has suffering built the perseverance and character that allows the infectious hope of eternity to grow in your life and spread into the lives of others?

CRAFT YOUR STORY

Write about a time in your life when you were suffering. How did God help you through that time? What did you learn about yourself through that experience? How did that part of your story help you grow in character and hope?

SHARE YOUR STORY

Find someone today who is suffering and do something for them to share the love and hope of Jesus.

LIVE YOUR STORY

Consider how you can use your experience with suffering to help others carry their own. What have you gone through in your life that Jesus wants you to use to help others?

NOTES

My Future, Your Glory

I read recently that our nation's levels of anxiety and worry about the future are at an all-time high. But I didn't need a news article to tell me that. With bad news swirling around us like the latest COVID variant, environmental crisis, war, and economic downturn, I can find myself feeling uneasy about the present and uncertain about the future. My wife tells me that when it comes to my outlook on the unknown parts of my future, I'm too often a worst-case-scenario kind of guy. I believe the term she's used in the past to describe my pessimistic outlook is "Negative Nelly." Have I saved enough money for retirement? Will interest rates ever go down? What if I get sick? Is my family going to be OK? If left to my own thoughts and worries, negative can become my new normal.

192 MY STORY, YOUR GLORY

So how can we say that the future looks good even when so much in the world is trying to tell a different story? How can we trust that God has our tomorrow when we can't see the forest for the trees today?

I once spoke with a fellow musician about our respective journeys in music, the discouraging moments in our careers, and how those situations led to good things. I remember getting depressed when I moved to Nashville and was auditioning for a record deal. I am not kidding that I was turned down by every single record label and some of them, multiple times. Looking back on those days now, I can clearly see how the moments of rejection helped me discover my love for songwriting. And after four long years until I was finally signed, the very record label with which I signed my deal also introduced me to the woman I would marry. Looking back, it sure seems like those things happened just the ways they were supposed to. I wouldn't have it any other way. I guess sometimes the key to embracing the *future* is looking back at how the Master Storyteller has shaped your life in the past . . . even when you couldn't clearly see how He was working.

That is one of the major lessons in the Old Testament story of Joseph. As we've discussed, Joseph's life is such a wild roller-coaster ride with twists and turns and ups and downs. He's thrown into a pit by his brothers and sold into slavery. He's falsely accused of a crime and sent to prison. But God uses all these events to make him the right-hand man of Egypt's king, Pharaoh. At the very end of the Joseph story, we find an incredible moment when his brothers apologize for leaving him for dead and selling him into slavery. Joseph tells them, "You intended to harm me, but God intended it for good to accomplish what is now being done, the saving of many lives" (Genesis 50:20).

Wow! What would it be like to look at even the most challenging moments of our life and know that God is going to use them for good in the future?

So when you are faced with times of uncertainty and confusion about the future, gain a different perspective by choosing to turn around and face the past. Remind yourself of God's faithfulness yesterday to help calm your anxiousness about tomorrow. The knowledge that God has brought you this far can move your heart from constant worry to holy anticipation, from anxiety to wonder, from disappointment to discovery, from grumbling to gratitude.

Maybe the best way to live our story for His Glory is to wake up every day and expect that God is doing great things even when we can't see them in the moment. When you give your future to God, you ensure that your future will ultimately give glory to God. You see, the future should be exciting when you know that the author of your life is the Master Storyteller, who knows the plans He has for you.

CONNECT TO HIS STORY

Read the following passage and consider how it applies to your life:

GENESIS 41:1-14 *"When two full years had passed, Pharaoh had a dream: He was standing by the Nile, when out of the river there came up seven cows, sleek and fat, and they grazed among the reeds. After them, seven other cows, ugly and gaunt, came up out of the Nile and stood beside those on the riverbank. And the cows that were ugly and gaunt ate up the seven sleek, fat cows. Then Pharaoh woke up. He fell asleep again and had a second dream: Seven heads of grain, healthy and good, were growing on a single stalk. After them, seven other heads of grain sprouted—thin and scorched by the east wind. The thin heads of grain swallowed up the seven healthy, full heads. Then Pharaoh woke up; it had been a dream. In the morning his mind was troubled, so he sent for all the magicians and wise men of Egypt. Pharaoh told them his dreams, but no one could interpret them for him. Then the chief cupbearer said to Pharaoh, 'Today I am reminded of my shortcomings. Pharaoh was once angry with his servants, and he imprisoned me and the chief baker in the house of the captain of the guard. Each of us had a dream the same night, and each dream had a meaning of its own. Now a young Hebrew was there with us, a servant of the captain of the guard. We told him our dreams, and he interpreted them for us, giving each man the interpretation of his dream. And*

> *things turned out exactly as he interpreted them to us: I was*
> *restored to my position, and the other man was impaled.' So,*
> *Pharaoh sent for Joseph, and he was quickly brought from*
> *the dungeon. When he had shaved and changed his clothes,*
> *he came before Pharaoh."*

In what ways can you relate to the unexpected ups and downs of Joseph's story?

In this passage Joseph is called out of prison after two years of waiting, all because of his God-given ability to interpret dreams. Can you identify with being faithful and waiting on God to do something in your life?

What does Joseph's greater story have to teach us about how God works in our lives and how we should view our future?

CRAFT YOUR STORY

Today spend some time thinking about three instances when God was faithful in your past. Write about how these moments of faithfulness can give you strength to approach the future with hope and anticipation.

SHARE YOUR STORY

One of the beautiful things about Christian community is how God uses us to help each other see His work of grace in our lives. Take some time to write a note to someone today who is experiencing difficulties and may need to be reminded of God's faithfulness in their life. Another way to be an encouragement to others is to share your story of God's faithfulness at popwe.org.

LIVE YOUR STORY

Pray about one area of the future that causes you the most fear and anxiety. Try to go throughout your day focused on the truth that God is working in ways you cannot see. Walk into those situations with expectation, asking, "What's next, Father?"

NOTES

My Hope, Your Glory

You only have to turn on the local news to embrace a stark reality: we desperately need a place called heaven. The world isn't perfect; in fact, the older I get, the more I realize there is a lot in this broken world that only heaven will set right. I'll never forget the moments I spent writing a song alongside my friend Mike Weaver from the band Big Daddy Weave. We got together just months after Mike had tragically lost his brother Jay. It was an emotional time for him and his family, and we did way more talking than writing that day. But our conversations about grief and loss led to a beautiful song called "Heaven Changes Everything." I will always remember how our conversations that day touched on this powerful truth: if there were no promise of heaven, then our tears would continue to flow, our deepest questions would never find answers, and all our last goodbyes would be final. The promise of heaven really does change everything.

Embracing the reality of heaven will even transform the way we live our lives in this present moment. During the pandemic in 2020, I found myself writing a lot of songs about heaven—it was a season of longing, reflection, and grief for a lot of us. Many of those tunes were lamentations, kind of like the one I wrote with Casting Crowns, "Scars in Heaven." But as I studied the Bible during that season, God laid on my heart that I also needed to write a song *rejoicing* about the promise of heaven. The promise of trumpets sounding, tears being wiped away, and sickness healed. I needed a celebration of what's to come—the home that Jesus promises us.

I looked to the New Testament and the moments where Jesus talked specifically about heaven. As He hung on the cross, in the midst of excruciating suffering, Jesus told one of the criminals next to Him to get ready for paradise. "Paradise" . . . what a wonderful description of eternal life. Jesus's depth of absolute grace for a criminal who probably didn't have a lifetime of good deeds and never got a chance to turn from his life of crime— simply believing in Jesus was enough. In the Gospel of John, Jesus is talking about heaven when He says, "I go and prepare a *place* for you" (14:3). He uses the Greek word *topos*, which in the ancient language refers to a real, physical place. Jesus isn't being metaphorical. Jesus uses real physical references that reflect tangible spaces such as "rooms" and "house" to describe heaven.

I have found that having that *eternal* mindset is a monumental shift that literally changes everything about the way we live our life. In the light of eternity, does this petty little argument I'm having with my coworker really matter? In light of eternity, is it OK for me to stay silent about my faith and not try to reach my unsaved friends and family? In the light of eternity, does it make sense for me to be placing so much priority on my work and on earning more money? In light of eternity, how can I possibly not feed the hungry and care for the poor?

If I understand the truth of heaven, shouldn't I be quick to forgive? If I take Jesus at His word, can't I look forward to a sweet reunion with the loved ones I have lost? In light of Jesus's promise, can't I hope for an eternity where everything is set right?

Questions such as these tend to find a new answer quickly when our eyes are fixed on heaven and the promise that our stories live forever. It is hard to truly live freely without embracing the truth that *everything* is going to be set right. The more mindful I am of the celebration to come, the more I live my life with the anticipation of that party in paradise. The truth of heaven transforms the daily focus of my life from the temporary to the eternal. We can live a truer story when our eyes are looking toward our true home.

CONNECT TO HIS STORY

Read the following passages and consider how they apply to your life:

> **JOHN 14:1-6** *"Do not let your hearts be troubled. You believe in God; believe also in me. My Father's house has many rooms; if that were not so, would I have told you that I am going there to prepare a place for you? And if I go and prepare a place for you, I will come back and take you to be with me that you also may be where I am. You know the way to the place where I am going.' Thomas said to him, 'Lord, we don't know where you are going, so how can we know the way?' Jesus answered, 'I am the way and the truth and the life. No one comes to the Father except through me.'"*

> **LUKE 23:43** *"Jesus answered him, 'Truly I tell you, today you will be with me in paradise.'"*

In these passages, how do Jesus's words about heaven give you hope today?

What does it mean to you that Jesus promises the criminal next to him that he would see "paradise"? What does it say about God's grace? What does it say about heaven that Jesus calls it paradise?

When Jesus says that He goes to "prepare a place for you," does it change the way you see your day-to-day struggles, your losses, your victories? What does it mean to you that Jesus says His Father has "many rooms"?

CRAFT YOUR STORY

Spend some time thinking about heaven and reflecting on the Scriptures in this devotion. Write about how your story may change when you keep the eternal perspective at the front of your mind.

SHARE YOUR STORY

Share what the hope of heaven means to you today in this moment with your family, small group, accountability partner, or a friend.

LIVE YOUR STORY

Write down three decisions that you will make differently as you consider them in light of eternity. Maybe you'll address a life choice, a relationship, or a work-related decision. How can you allow the truth of heaven to change the direction of your life right now? Place these three decisions in your desk drawer and set a reminder to revisit them in a month. Then consider how God has used these choices to change you, your family, or community.

NOTES

ACKNOWLEDGMENTS

Thanks to Matt Litton for partnering with me to create a book that I believe God is going to use to speak to people in a powerful way.

Thanks to Dave Schroeder, Steve Green, WTA, and Story House Collective for being on the team. And thank *you* for reading this book. I hope it inspires you to make the most of the one life you get. It's your story for His Glory!

—MW

ABOUT THE AUTHOR

Matthew West is a five-time GRAMMY® nominee, a multiple ASCAP Christian Music Songwriter of the Year winner, and a 2018 Dove Award Songwriter of the Year recipient. He has received an American Music Award, a Billboard Music Award, and a K-LOVE Fan Award and was named *Billboard*'s Hot Christian Songwriter of the Year. A recipient of the Rich Mullins Impact Award, West also received a Primetime Emmy® Award nomination for Original Music & Lyrics for the title track for the feature film *The Heart of Christmas*. He has been awarded an RIAA Gold certifications for his singles "Hello, My Name Is," "Broken Things," and "Strong Enough," and RIAA Platinum certification for the songs "The Motions" and "My Jesus."

In addition to his own recording career, he has cohosted the K-LOVE Fan Awards five times and has more than two hundred songwriting credits to his name, including cuts by Casting Crowns, Rascal Flatts, Anne Wilson, Michael W. Smith, Amy Grant, Scotty McCreery, Danny Gokey, and others, racking up thirty No. 1 songs.

Adding author to his list of accolades, West has written six books to date: *Give This Christmas Away*, *The Story of Your Life*, *Forgiveness*, *Today Is Day One*, *Hello, My Name Is*, and his latest before this title, *The God Who Stays*. He is also passionate about providing hope and healing through the power of prayer and story. Along with his father, Pastor Joe West, they founded popwe, a nonprofit ministry helping others to craft, share, and live a more meaningful life. Please visit popwe.org for more information.

Matt Litton is a writer and bestselling collaborator with three No. 1 *Publishers Weekly* and *Wall Street Journal* non-fiction bestselling books. His most recent projects include *The God Who Stays* by Matthew West (with Matt Litton), K-Love Fan Award–winning devotional *On Our Knees* by Phil Wickham (with Matt Litton), and the coauthored forty-day contemplative devotional titled *In the Presence of Jesus* by Paul Bane and Matt Litton. Matt resides in Nashville with his wife and family. You can read more about Matt and his work at www.mattlitton.com.

Stay up to date on music, tours & more at
MATTHEWWEST.COM

For more information about Matthew's ministry pop**we** visit pop**we**.org

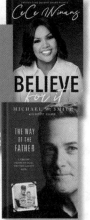